Gallica

Volume 53

VERGINIA, LUCRETIA, AND THE MEDIEVAL LIVY

Gallica

ISSN 1749-091X

Founding Editor: Sarah Kay

Series Editors: Peggy McCracken, Miranda Griffin

Gallica aims to provide a forum for the best current work in medieval and early modern French studies. Literary studies are particularly welcome and preference is given to works written in English, although publication in French is not excluded.

Proposals or queries should be sent in the first instance to the editors, or to the publisher, at the addresses given below; all submissions receive prompt and informed consideration.

Professor Miranda Griffin (mhg11@cam.ac.uk)
Professor Peggy McCracken (peggymcc@umich.edu)
Caroline Palmer (editorial@boydell.co.uk)

Previously published volumes in this series are listed at the end of this volume

VERGINIA, LUCRETIA, AND THE MEDIEVAL LIVY

AN EDITION AND TRANSLATION OF EPISODES FROM PIERRE BERSUIRE'S *TITE-LIVE* AND JEAN DE MEUN'S *ROMAN DE LA ROSE*

EDITED BY NOAH D. GUYNN, DAVID F. HULT,
AND ELIZABETH SCALA

D. S. BREWER

First published 2025
D. S. Brewer, Cambridge

ISBN 978-1-84384-735-9

D. S. Brewer is an imprint of Boydell & Brewer Ltd
PO Box 9, Woodbridge, Suffolk IP12 3DF, UK
and of Boydell & Brewer Inc.
668 Mt Hope Avenue, Rochester, NY 14620–2731, USA
website: www.boydellandbrewer.com

A CIP catalogue record for this book is available
from the British Library

The publisher has no responsibility for the continued existence or accuracy of
URLs for external or third-party internet websites referred to in this book, and
does not guarantee that any content on such websites is, or will remain, accurate
or appropriate

Please note that some of the discussion in this book addresses sensitive issues
including rape

CONTENTS

ACKNOWLEDGMENTS

This project has been delightfully collaborative, especially so since it began during lockdown in 2020. Our edition and translation would not have been possible without the generosity of several colleagues at far-flung institutions remote from our own.

First, we wish to thank Daniel Wakelin, Jeremy Griffiths Professor of Medieval Palaeography at the University of Oxford, who went on two occasions to the Bodleian Library and took exquisite digital photographs of the relevant pages of Rawlinson C 447 for us. While that manuscript can now be found online at Digital Bodleian, when we began the project it could not.

We are also grateful to Ina Nettekoven at Dr. Jörn Günther Rare Books in Basel, Switzerland for providing us with access to, and permission to reproduce, pen-and-wash drawings from a paper manuscript of the First Decade of the *Tite-Live* that was produced in Lille ca. 1470. (See the "Notes on Images," below.)

Next, we wish to thank classicist and Livy expert Timothy Moore at Washington University, St. Louis for reading our text and notes with remarkable rigor and insight. His suggestions and corrections proved invaluable and prevented a number of errors.

Finally, we are grateful to the anonymous readers for the press for offering us precious feedback on our work; to the editors of the Gallica Series, Miranda Griffin and Peggy McCracken, for their interest in our project; and to Caroline Palmer and Laura Bennetts of Boydell & Brewer, for shepherding our manuscript through peer review and production.

FIGURES

The editors, contributors, and publisher are grateful to all the institutions and persons listed for permission to reproduce the materials in which they hold copyright. Every effort has been made to trace the copyright holders; apologies are offered for any omission, and the publisher will be pleased to add any necessary acknowledgment in subsequent editions.

INTRODUCTION

This book began with the need to write a footnote, part of a small project to understand better Chaucer's "Physician's Tale," a retelling of the story of Verginia that fits somewhat unsurely into the larger *Canterbury Tales*.[1] Like the Lucretia episode, with which it is often associated, this story of sexual predation, tragic death, and Roman heroism emotionally rouses its audience. Yet it also remains confused both by the medieval Christian context in which it is retold as well as by materials Chaucer's narrator adds to its disturbing central episode, in which a father kills his own child to prevent her violation. The Physician calls Livy his source, but he offers no slavish or even faithful imitation of the classical narrative. Much gets changed. Descriptions, details, and biblical allusions are added as the Physician transforms Livy's highly political narrative of Verginius's heroism into a story of female moral virtue. What had seemed at first a simple translation unveils a story of interwoven materials and intellectual circles in at least three languages – Latin, French, and English – with few unobstructed lines of influence.

Chaucer's readers have long recognized the *Roman de la rose* as the poet's more proximate source for this story, particularly because of the unusual manner of Verginia's death, which Jean de Meun seems to have invented. In a narrative much stripped down from the Latin original, Jean's Verginius beheads his daughter in place of the furtive stabbing in the Roman forum that Livy dramatizes. Yet Jean cannot be Chaucer's only source. The "Physician's Tale" also includes details that Jean's does not, details derived either from Livy or from a source directly familiar with the Roman historian. One such source might be his London contemporary and friend, John Gower, who tells the story of Verginia in book 7 of his Middle English story-collection *Confessio Amantis*, in a segment devoted to the "education of the king." In the *Confessio*, the Verginia story directly follows Lucretia's and shares a number of details with Livy. Offering no evidence of having used Jean's *Rose*, Gower's Verginia is killed, as in the Latin source, with a knife "thurgh

---

[1] See Elizabeth Scala, "Did Chaucer Know Livy?" *Notes & Queries* 68 (September 2021): 1–4.

his dowhter side" (7.5245). However, no one clear line of influence moves us from Livy's history to the "Physician's Tale." Chaucer's departures from Jean's and Gower's very different source materials suggest that some version of Livy was circulating in London at the time Gower and Chaucer were writing, perhaps influencing the English poets independently.

Research into the circulation of Livian materials leads to the work of Pierre Bersuire, who completed his *Decades de Tite-Live*, a French translation of Livy's history of Rome, *Ab urbe condita* (*From the Founding of the City*), sometime between 1354 and 1358. The translation, one of the earliest renderings of a classical text into a European vernacular, was commissioned by King John II of France, Jean le Bon, soon after his accession to the throne in 1350. Its author was an encyclopedist well known in medieval literary circles, including English ones, for his commentaries, homilies, and sermons. Born in Poitou, Bersuire entered a Franciscan order as a young man before becoming a Benedictine and moving to Avignon. He resided for twelve years at the papal court, where he encountered Petrarch and worked for Cardinal Peter de Pratis, a papal vice-chancellor. While in Avignon, he also wrote the *Reductorium morale*, the majority of which is a moralization of the *De proprietatibus rerum*, an encyclopedia of the natural world by Bartholomeus Anglicus. The *Reductorium* is a text offering multiple, sometimes contradictory, moral allegorizations of the stories it collects, presumably for preachers.[2] Book XV of this long work circulated independently in the Middle Ages as the *Ovidius moralizatus*, a moralization of Ovid's *Metamorphoses* rendered in Latin prose. That text, which has recently received a new edition and English translation,[3] has long been acknowledged as a source for other stories written by Chaucer and Gower.

Bersuire's literary credentials are impressive and extend well beyond the *Ovidius*, for which he is now almost exclusively known. He spent the latter part of his life in Paris, initially studying at the university, where he again encountered Petrarch. He then served, from 1354 on, as the Prior of Saint-Eloy de Paris on the Île de la Cité. It is here that Bersuire wrote the *Tite-Live*, at the behest of Jean le Bon (see Figure 1). Like his previous work, the *Tite-Live* signals to us that Bersuire belongs to the humanist circles with which we more readily associate figures like Petrarch and Dante. His work pivots toward the classics both in the way that the *Reductorium* puts the mysteries of scripture, the natural world, and the fables of the poets "on the same footing,"

----

    [2]   See Ralph Hexter, "The *Allegari* of Pierre Bersuire: Interpretation and the *Reductorium Morale*," *Allegorica* 10 (1989): 51–84.
    [3]   Pierre Bersuire, *The Moralized Ovid*, ed. and trans. Frank T. Coulson and Justin Haynes (Cambridge, MA: Dumbarton Oaks Medieval Library, Harvard University Press, 2023).

Figure 1 Pierre Bersuire presenting the *Tite-Live* to Jean le Bon.
A privately held Lillois manuscript, ca. 1470, f. 10r. Courtesy Dr. Jörn Günther
Rare Books, Basel (Switzerland).

to quote Ralph Hexter,[4] and in the way that the *Tite-Live* expresses reverence for Livy's refined diction and learned latinity ("tres haute maniere de parler et la parfonde latinité"),[5] which he is at pains to imitate and understand.

Full acceptance of Bersuire's *Tite-Live* as the English poets' primary source has not yet occurred, largely for two (related) reasons. First, the few scholars who have compared Bersuire to Chaucer and to Livy's Latin have found no smoking gun: no detail or wording in the French that would prove incontrovertibly that his translation was his source. Because Bersuire was a faithful translator of Livy's Latin, they insist that, since nothing in Bersuire cannot also be found in Livy himself, we should take writers like Chaucer and Gower at their word when they claim their tales come from "Titus Livius." But a second, practical consideration hinders such comparison. There is no modern edition of Bersuire's French text and no full English translation to consult, making any case about Bersuire's intervention that much harder to pursue. We have either had to take matters on the authority of the few scholars who have dipped into the early incunable printings of Bersuire's French translation, which offer a corrected and further edited version of his text, or we have had to make recourse to modern editions of Livy himself – scholarly gestures that both silently maintain the status quo.

The frustrations of this situation led to the inception of the present work: an edition and translation of the entire Verginia story from an early manuscript of the *Tite-Live* – Bodleian MS Rawlinson C 447 – that is proximate to Bersuire's own writing and that presents a more authoritative text than the incunabula, which were made from later, revised manuscripts. This manuscript offers a version of Bersuire's Livy closest to what might have been in circulation in Chaucer's and Gower's London. Rawlinson C 447 has been identified as a copy representing the earliest stages of transmission for the *Tite-Live*. It is what Marie-Hélène Tesnière calls "un exemplaire de travail" ("a working copy"),[6] and it contains Bersuire's own work rather than the later reception of his translation, which was much influenced by the editorial work carried out by the intellectual program of Jean le Bon's son, Charles V. Indeed, according to Tesnière, only this manuscript and one other, BnF nafr. 27401, can be

---

4   Hexter, "The *Allegari* of Pierre Bersuire," 62.

5   The quotations are from Bersuire's prologue to the *Tite-Live*, which Marie-Hélène Tesnière cites in extenso in "Pierre Bersuire, traducteur des *Décades* de Tite-Live: Nouvelles Perspectives," in *Quand les auteurs étaient des nains: Stratégies auctoriales des traducteurs français de la fin du Moyen Âge*, ed. Olivier Delsaux and Tania Van Hemelryck (Turnhout: Brepols, 2019), p. 115 [113–58].

6   Tesnière, "À propos de la traduction de Tite-Live par Pierre Bersuire: Le manuscrit Oxford, Bibliothèque Bodléienne Rawlinson C 447," *Romania* 118 (2000): 450 [449–98].

considered Bersuire's because the revisions and emendations made later were so substantial.[7]

To give context to the Verginia narrative in Bersuire, we decided to add an edition and translation of Bersuire's Lucretia episode to the project. The counterpoint between the stories is relevant for a number of reasons. The stories are linked explicitly by Livy's reference back to Lucretia at the opening of the Verginia episode, which likely evolved out of the Lucretia episode in the first place. Both are narratives of political revolt important to Roman republicanism, and both hinge on acts of sexual violence, real or planned, perpetrated against chaste women. Aristocratic Lucretia commits suicide after her rape by Tarquin the Proud, precipitating the downfall of the monarchy and the establishment of the Roman Republic. Plebeian Verginia is murdered by her father, who prefers to see her die free than be seized as a slave by the corrupt judge Appius. Verginia's death then inspires a mass uprising that overthrows the decemvirs, a body of ten republican officials who abuse the very laws they have codified. Both stories illustrate political corruption threatening Rome and signal the city's integrity and political renewal through the bodies of two chaste women. While the stories threaten female virtue – *pudicitia* – with male sexual aggression, they also answer it with death, a preferred end to the shame of such corruption. Yet the stories are not equally "about" Roman women, even if they could be shaped as such by the medieval poets interested in using them as exempla of Christian virtues. In Livy, Lucretia is a well-developed heroic figure in a surprisingly economical narrative, and her own concern for her shame and legacy governs her story. By contrast, Verginia is a passive, silent figure around whom a great deal of heroic action and speech-making occurs. Her father, Verginius, is cast as the central character, and the story extolls his Roman heroism. Even Icilius, Verginia's betrothed, plays a greater part than Verginia, speaking in her father's absence and in her defense because she cannot.

These moving stories of quasi-"saintly" women – women who were sacrificed and seemed to accept death – were adapted to Christian ethics in various medieval texts by restyling them as examples of chastity and virginity. Those virtues were valued by Christian culture in ways distinct from the political heroism favored by the Romans, possibly because suicide and child-murder were difficult to condone as forms of Christian heroism. Medieval retellings of these stories were common, though direct access to Livy was difficult, particularly in England, where manuscripts of his history were rare. The vast majority were (and remain) in Italian and French libraries. However, the medieval retellings of these stories suggest a complex circulation of Livian materials and layers of classical reception that have too often been

---

[7]   Tesnière, "Pierre Bersuire, traducteur des *Décades* de Tite-Live," p. 144.

simplified when they have not been ignored. Moreover, in the English tradition particularly, Bersuire has yet to be fully recognized, as he is in France, for his part in the transmission of Livy's history and in the development of the late medieval humanism in which his translation is embedded. The fact that Bersuire's is among the earliest vernacular translations of any classical text should on its own be enough to prompt more attention to this work.

Tracing Livy's influence in medieval Europe is challenging because of the relative scarcity of manuscripts of *Ab urbe condita*.[8] Setting aside Jean de Meun, whose attention to Livy was unusually early, it is only around 1300 that sustained interest in *Ab urbe condita* developed and that a commentary and translation tradition began in earnest.[9] Where today's scholars would like to disentangle Latin threads from vernacular ones, the warp of Latin textual transmission remains entwined in the weft of scholastic commentary, vernacular citation, and quotation. There is no developmental line that transitions neatly from one language to another, as if in some idealized *translatio studii et imperii*. Admired by Petrarch, who worked on collecting, collating, and correcting Livy manuscripts in the early part of his career, Bersuire haunted intellectual circles in Paris and Avignon, both royal and curial households; and his connections to the papal court likely provided the source materials for his translation of Livy done at royal behest.[10] But Bersuire also benefited from an earlier fourteenth-century commentary on Livy made by the English Dominican Nicholas Trevet for Pope John XXII. Both of these texts were commissioned by powerful men interested in the moral truths and heroic examples of Roman history but who presumably found the Latin difficult. They reveal a cultural milieu we have only observed piecemeal and perhaps too separate from the humanist interests of the later court of Charles V, who commissioned a number of French translations of Greek and Latin classics.

In *Inferno* 28, Dante famously calls Livy a writer "che non erra," though evidence that he knew Livy directly is slight. What we do know is that Livy's reputation was venerable and widespread. In encyclopedic sources like

---

[8]   Of the roughly 200 surviving manuscripts of the First Decade, "only 24 witnesses are from time periods earlier than the thirteenth century." See Marielle de Fanchis, "Livian Manuscript Tradition," in *A Companion to Livy*, ed. Bernard Mineo (Chichester: Wiley, 2015), p. 5 [3–23].

[9]   See Pierre Maréchaux, "The Transmission of Livy from the End of the Roman Empire to the Beginning of the Seventeenth Century," in *A Companion to Livy*, p. 440 [439–51].

[10]   For Petrarch's role in the textual transmission of Livy in the Middle Ages, see Giuseppe Billanovich, "Petrarch and the Textual Tradition of Livy," *Journal of the Warburg and Courtauld Institutes* 14 (1951): 137–208. For important modifications to Billanovich's conclusions see M. D. Reeve, "The Place of P in the Stemma of Livy 1–10," in *Medieval Manuscripts of the Latin Classics: Production and Use* (London: Red Gull Press, 1996), pp. 74–90. For the precise dating of the *Tite-Live*, see Tesnière, "Pierre Bersuire, traducteur des Decades de Tite-Live," esp. p. 134.

those of Fulgentius and Vincent of Beauvais, Livy's name circulated as the foremost authority on the history of Rome. Of course, Rome functioned as an important base for medieval European cultural identity. All western medieval monarchies traced their origins in some way to both Christian and legendary Rome. Given the explicitly anti-monarchial and pagan framework of these Roman origins, it might be a surprise to see popes and kings turning to Livy for exemplary narratives. But that seems to have been the case. In the lengthy prologue Bersuire appended to his translation, he explains why someone like Jean le Bon might wish to know Roman history. As Tesnière puts it, the goal was to "pérenniser la transmission de la Couronne de France et préserver l'intégrité du royaume dans le cadre d'une guerre juste."[11] Transmission of the French crown aligns with the transmission of Roman history through an analogy of just war.

The stories of female virtue that are our focus were a core component of Rome's foundational legends and the lineage of empire it grounds for European culture. Connected to each other by their Latin source, the stories of Lucretia and Verginia appeal in similar ways to medieval values, *mutatis mutandis*, of feminine chastity and purity. If the women's deaths were clarion calls to political action in the Roman past, their suffering bespoke ideals of feminine virtue in the medieval vernaculars and could be adapted to emotively-charged literary ends.

The popularity of the Lucretia story in the Middle Ages was extensive. Nearly every medieval vernacular retells the story of her rape and suicide. Beginning with Augustine, who ultimately condemns her for her despair, a steady line of writers and commentators make recourse to the Lucretia legend: Dante places her in limbo with other virtuous heathens in *Inferno* 4; Boccaccio retells her story heroically in *De mulieribus claris*; and Petrarch does so in both *Africa* and the *Trionfi*, where he yokes her with Verginia in the "triumph of chastity." Lucretia also makes an appearance in Chaucer's *Legend of Good Women*, Gower's *Confessio Amantis*, and Christine de Pizan's *Cité des dames*. These are only the best-known references to Lucretia in medieval vernacular literature; there are others too numerous to detail.

In contrast to Lucretia's ubiquity, Verginia appears more sporadically. None of the Augustinian commentaries that remark on Lucretia mentions Verginia.[12] Verginia's appearance, then, in Jean de Meun's portion of the *Roman de la rose*, as well as in Chaucer's "Physician's Tale" and Gower's *Confessio Amantis*, is all the more remarkable, attesting to a circulation of Livy in some form

---

[11] Tesnière, "Pierre Bersuire, traducteur des Decades de Tite-Live," p. 118.

[12] Andrew Galloway discusses these commentaries and their important interpretation of Lucretia's Roman behavior in strikingly historicist ways in "Chaucer's Legend of Lucrece and the Critique of Ideology in Fourteenth-Century England," *ELH* 30 (1993): 813–32.

between England and the Continent that has yet to be firmly traced. The early and dramatic way that Jean retells the Verginia story speaks to the interest in Livy appearing in the late thirteenth century, when Jean was "completing" Guillaume's *Rose* with encyclopedic and scholastic gusto. It is the first evidence of French interest in the Roman historian and, as has been noted, is a principal source of Chaucer's rendition. It also marks a beginning to a vernacular Livy tradition whose effects can be felt in commentary, translation, and adaptation. We thus have included Jean's Verginia and Lucretia narratives alongside Bersuire's in a presentation of the French reception of Livy in the late thirteenth century and early-to-mid fourteenth.

Jean's unusual interest in Verginia, which he presents as an example of the power of love over a justice that can be too easily corrupted, might be explained by the connections among intellectuals precisely at the moment of French political history in which Bersuire's translation of Livy was completed. Tesnière notes that the *Tite-Live* has a likely terminus ad quem of 1358, as attested by an explicit in BnF nafr. 27401 indicating that the translation was completed soon after September 21, 1358. This was a turbulent year, marking what Tesnière, citing historian Jacques Krynen, calls "la tourmente de la 'révolution parisienne.'"[13] Jean le Bon was being held prisoner in England following a defeat at Poitiers, and his regent, the dauphin and future Charles V, was being thwarted by the Estates General, by hostility from a rival to the throne, and by attacks from the Parisian burghers under the leadership of Étienne Marcel, the Provost of Merchants. When Marcel sought to impose limits on the king's fiscal authority, he precipitated a political crisis that led to a mob invading the royal palace on the Île de la Cité, directly across from Saint-Eloy. The mob murdered the marshals of Champagne and Normandy in front of the dauphin himself; and in a gesture meant to humiliate Charles, Marcel exchanged hats with him, placing the insurrectionists' *chaperon*, with its signature colors (*pers*, or dark blue, and red), on his head. The crisis eventually passed, as Marcel lost the support of the aristocracy and was murdered, likely on the orders of the burghers, who thought he had gone too far in opposing the monarchy. What is most compelling about this history for our purposes is that, as Tesnière notes, Saint-Eloy served as an arsenal and a gathering place for the insurrectionists, and the blue-and-red *chaperon* makes an appearance on the opening folio of BnF nafr. 27401 (see Figure 2a), crowning a marginal grotesque who plays the vielle (see Figure 2b).[14]

---

[13] Tesnière, "Pierre Bersuire, traducteur des Decades de Tite-Live," p. 134. See Jacques Krynen, "Entre la réforme et la révolution: Paris, 1356–1358," in *Les révolutions françaises: Les phénomènes révolutionnaires en France du Moyen Âge à nos jours*, ed. Frédéric Bluche (Paris: Fayard, 1989), pp. 87–112.

[14] Tesnière, "Pierre Bersuire, traducteur des Decades de Tite-Live," p. 135.

Figure 2b   Marginal grotesque, frontispiece detail, *Tite-Live*.
Bibliothèque nationale de France, Département des Manuscrits, nafr. 27401,
f. 1r, detail.

Tesnière's thesis is that Bersuire, under the influence of a figure like Nicole Oresme, Philippe de Vitry, or Guillaume de Machaut, had joined a group of reformers who were calling for a government more responsive to the "volonté du peuple" and the "commun consentement," terms that appear frequently in the reform vocabulary of the time.[15] She also sees indirect references to contemporary events in the marginal notes Bersuire adds to signal to his readers – starting with Jean le Bon himself – analogies between the revolts of the Roman plebs and the revolt of Marcel and the burghers.[16] Krynen gives an even fuller account of the role of Parisian intellectuals in the crisis of 1358, starting with the observation that medieval societies were well acquainted with the idea of negotiations between government and the governed and that

[15]   Tesnière, "Pierre Bersuire, traducteur des Decades de Tite-Live," p. 135, citing Krynen, "Le vocabulaire politique en France à la fin du Moyen Âge: L'idée de réformation," in *État et Église dans la genèse de l'État moderne: Actes du colloque organisé par le CNRS et la Casa de Velázquez, Madrid, 30 novembre et 1er décembre 1984*, ed. Jean-Philippe Genet and Bernard Vincent (Madrid: Casa de Velázquez, 1986), pp. 145–64.
[16]   Tesnière, "Pierre Bersuire, traducteur des Decades de Tite-Live," p. 137.

medieval thinkers derived a notion of constitutional guarantees of liberty and privileges from ancient thinkers, notably Aristotle. These ideas have little to do with modern democracy, just as the revolt of the burghers bears little resemblance to modern revolutions. Still, for Krynen, the revolt would not have happened at all without a political theory behind it, specifically a theory that was widespread in medieval secular and ecclesiastical assemblies and that was encapsulated in a motto derived from Roman civil law: "quod omnes tangit ab omnibus tractari et approbari debet" ("that which concerns all must be discussed and approved by all").[17]

If Tesnière is right that Bersuire belongs to the intellectual culture that asked royal power to submit to the rights of the community, then the *Tite-Live* can perhaps be read as an effort to mobilize Roman history – and specifically the rebellions against royal and judicial tyranny that occur in the Verginia and Lucretia episodes – on behalf of a reform movement. That movement sought to guarantee the rights of the governed to negotiate the terms of their subjection and envisioned social cohesion as dependent upon such rights. Krynen suggests that if it were not for the work of intellectuals like Oresme, who was a friend and confidant to Charles V and translated Aristotle's *Ethics* and *Politics* at his bidding, these ideas about governance and cohesion might not have had an afterlife beyond the mid-fourteenth century.[18] We might add that Bersuire played his own role in the transmission of reformist ideas and, like Oresme, did so through translation. The difference is that the work he translated was not a philosophical treatise but a history of Rome, one that used gripping episodes of threatened female virtue to signal – and defend – republican renewal.

In this complex and somewhat indirect way, we can situate Bersuire within early humanist circles with which we are not used to associating him and with early humanist conceptions of historiography that emphasize secularization without abandoning a theological conception of historical events and actors. Unlike his friend Petrarch, Bersuire tends to be regarded merely as a "scholastic," at least in English studies, largely on the basis of the title of the *Ovidius moralizatus* rather than any deep familiarity with that text or Bersuire's career. Yet Bersuire's scrupulous attention to language and stylistic detail, including the glossary with which he opens the *Tite-Live*, reveals a sophisticated effort at historicization of the classical materials before him. Where some have claimed that Bersuire renders Livy in a literal and workmanlike way, his glossary and prologue reveal an attention to Livy's abstruse language and style that tests his skills as a translator and Latinist. (By contrast, Bersuire's French is limpidly clear when writing his own material.) Our translation attempts an analogous faithfulness, capturing Bersuire's

---

[17] See Krynen, "Entre la réforme et la révolution," pp. 101–07.
[18] See Krynen, "Entre la réforme et la revolution," pp. 107–11.

imitation of Livy's intricate, knotty Latin prose style, rather than trying to turn Bersuire's work back into Livy's own. Our work is thus based on the premise that the *Tite-Live* is itself valuable, attesting to the rich cultural and political environments in which Bersuire worked, including curial offices and royal courts interested in conquest, empire, and just rule.

Across our edition and translation, we have struggled with the presentation of a number of historical, linguistic, and thematic issues. Some of our struggles imitate Bersuire's as he brings the classical world to his medieval audience. Others emerge from the cultural sensitivities of our present moment. The Verginia and Lucretia episodes are both about sexual aggression and violence, which is no less fraught in the various time periods in question than it is in our own. However, even more uncomfortable – and thus in need of discussion – are the uses to which such accounts may be put and the political and artistic interests they ultimately serve. No matter the historical era in which they are "heard," the voices of the women involved in these stories are muffled when they are not entirely silenced. The problem rears its head when we attempt to render the terms for sexual violation in these episodes into modern English, potentially blunting or overdramatizing the force of such acts in an effort at an historical representation of each writer's act of representation of such violence. Even when dedicated to the literal, are we to be faithful to the ways in which Livy (in classical Rome) or Bersuire (rendering classical Rome for a fourteenth-century French audience) writes – or, alternately, sensitive to modern audiences facing these different contexts from the vantage point of the present?

The term Livy uses for the designs on Verginia is a case in point: *stuprum*, which in classical Latin is an arresting word for what Appius desires to do. It combines shame, disgrace, defilement, violation, and dishonor in its transmission of a gross misconduct and lack of self-control. Rendering that term in English as "spoiling," as it often is, sounds much like a euphemism, even as it captures the very different familial and civic concerns that were pressing in Livy's Rome, where honor and freedom were potentially more important than the protective feeling we imagine a father should "naturally" have for his child. The ways in which these two cultures thought about such protections are radically at odds. We have here rendered Bersuire's *stupre* powerfully as "rape" whenever an act of forced intercourse is made explicit, as in the case of Lucretia. For Verginia we have been more cautious, in part because the crime is contemplated but not carried out. We have discussed our rationale further in the notes. More generally, the struggle with sense versus style in our modern translation, then, repeats these writers' struggles with decorum and valence in at least three separate historico-cultural contexts that are in need of far more consideration.

NOTES ON THE EDITION

Some sixty or more manuscripts of all or significant parts of Bersuire's *Tite-Live* have survived, the majority of which were copied in the fifteenth century, though a certain number of them were copied in the fourteenth century, some very close to the time the work was written.[1] Our knowledge of the manuscript tradition has been greatly enhanced by the publications of Marie-Hélène Tesnière over the past several decades.[2] As Tesnière makes it clear, only two manuscripts represent exemplars of Bersuire's initial version of the translation, whereas all the others contain a revised version of the history under the influence of King John II's successor, his eldest son who would become King Charles V, Charles le Sage, after John's death in 1364. As has recently been asserted, Bersuire's was, in its much better known and widely circulated revised version, "une œuvre de traduction capitale pour l'histoire des traductions et pour l'histoire des idées, dans la mesure où, une fois entré dans la Librairie de Charles V, l'exemplaire concerné fut orné de magnifiques miniatures. L'ouvrage aura une influence considérable sur la pensée et la politique de Charles V."[3]

---

[1] See Charles Samaran, "Pierre Bersuire, prieur de Saint-Éloi de Paris," *Histoire littéraire de la France* 39 (1962): 259–450. Jacques Monfrin, who contributed the section of Samaran's article on "La traduction française de Tite-Live" (358–414), summarizes the circulation of the translation as follows: "C'est à partir de la fin du XIVe siècle que la traduction de Bersuire s'est répandue" (406).

[2] The principal works by Tesnière we have consulted and to which we refer below are, in chronological order: "À propos de la traduction de Tite-Live par Pierre Bersuire: Le manuscrit Oxford, Bibliothèque Bodléienne Rawlinson C 447," *Romania* 118 (2000): 449–98; "Un manuscrit exceptionnel des *Décades* de Tite-Live traduites par Pierre Bersuire," in *La traduction vers le moyen français*, ed. Claudio Galderisi and Cinzia Pignatelli (Turnhout: Brepols, 2008), pp. 149–64; and "Pierre Bersuire, traducteur des *Décades* de Tite-Live: Nouvelles Perspectives," in *Quand les auteurs étaient des nains: Stratégies auctoriales des traducteurs français de la fin du Moyen Âge*, ed. Olivier Delsaux and Tania Van Hemelryck (Turnhout: Brepols, 2019), pp. 115–58.

[3] Charles Brucker, *Anthologie commentée des traductions françaises du XIVe siècle: Autour de Charles V (culture, pouvoir et spiritualité)*, 2 vols. (Paris: Champion, 2020), vol. 1, p. 334.

Concerning Bersuire's initial translation: classicists know of four parts of Livy's historical work that have come down to us, each part referred to as a "decade," in other words a collection of ten books. The second of these decades was not known in the Middle Ages, so the three decades that Bersuire translated, known to us as decades one, three, and four, were considered to be the total three decades of Livy's work. In an inventory of the sixty manuscripts of Bersuire's translation, Jacques Monfrin and Charles Samaran indicate that about one half are complete. The other half have only one or two of the decades, undoubtedly due to losses in these manuscripts' history.[4] The two manuscripts that Tesnière refers to as the earliest ones, and the closest to Bersuire's initial translation, are both ones that represent only a part of the whole. The one that Tesnière described years ago as an "exemplaire de travail," Rawlinson C 447, which is unlike any of the other manuscripts in having no illuminated miniatures and no luxury features, contains only the first decade. The second one, which was only discovered less than twenty years ago when the Bibliothèque nationale de France acquired it at auction (now BnF nafr. 27401), is, Tesnière asserts, the dedication copy of the final product, since its decoration dates it to about 1360 and the dedication copy could only be presented to King John in late 1360 or early 1361, when he was freed from his captivity in England after having been captured in the disastrous Battle of Poitiers. Furthermore, one of the two scribes of this manuscript is identified by Tesnière as a copyist known for his royal commissions during this period.[5] This manuscript is fragmented but is also the product of a poor binding job: it starts with a long, nearly complete, part of decade four, followed by a fragmented portion of the first decade (containing only the first four books). For our purposes in this edition, the texts regarding Verginia and Lucretia, found respectively in book three and book one of the first decade, are transmitted in these two manuscripts; and we have decided to use the Oxford manuscript (siglum *O*) as our base with, as control manuscripts where the reading of the Oxford manuscript is faulty, BnF nafr. 27401 (siglum *J*) and Paris, Bibliothèque Sainte-Geneviève 777 (siglum *G*). The latter is one of the early, sumptuous manuscripts of the "revised version," which was Charles V's personal exemplar and probably copied in the 1370s.

What are the major differences between, on the one hand, the two early manuscripts containing versions undoubtedly close to the translation by

---

[4]   See Samaran, "Pierre Bersuire," 434–50, a bibliography of manuscripts and editions to which Monfrin also contributed. The list of surviving complete manuscripts shows that because of the work's considerable length, amounting to hundreds of folios, it was frequently bound in two, three, or four volumes, loss of which could explain the number of incomplete exemplars that have survived.

[5]   Tesnière, "Un manuscrit exceptionnel," p. 150.

Bersuire and, on the other, manuscripts based upon the revised version, which rapidly became the only one that circulated in the late fourteenth and the fifteenth centuries? In an article devoted to the Oxford manuscript and published prior to the discovery of the dedication copy, Tesnière characterizes the stunning difference between its textual and physical properties and those of all the remaining manuscripts. To begin with, whereas all the other manuscripts are luxury products undoubtedly intended for a wealthy aristocratic audience, the Oxford manuscript is a "modest" exemplar, using thick, poorly prepared parchment and lacking any illuminated miniatures. Tesnière, perhaps rightly, associates the Oxford manuscript with a manuscript described as follows in the 1373 inventory of Charles V's library compiled by a certain Gilles Malet: "L'original de Titus Livius en françois, la premiere translacion qui en fu faite, escript de mauvese lettre, mal enluminé et point ystorié" ("The original copy of Livy in French, the first translation to have been made of it, poorly transcribed, badly decorated and not containing any illustrations of the narrative"). She also points out dialectal vocabulary in this manuscript that comes from Bersuire's birthplace, the West of France (Poitou and the Vendée) – vocabulary that was clearly not understood by the later copyists or, at the very least, that they replaced with more common French terms. As opposed to the Oxford manuscript, the dedication copy is a luxury product with abundant decoration and a couple of illustrations, though not a full "iconographic cycle," as found in the later manuscripts of the revised version. But its text, very close to that of the Oxford manuscript, also includes its dialectal vocabulary.

Another important difference that isolates these two manuscripts from the others is the nature of their divisions in the text. The Oxford manuscript divides each book into chapters, the numbers of which are rubricated in the margin. The chapters are themselves divided into "paragraphs" that are signaled by colored "pieds de mouche," or paragraph markers. Moreover, the paragraphs are numbered in red ink in the margin next to each of the markers. The dedication copy has for the most part the same chapter and paragraph divisions as the Oxford manuscript, but the numbering is lacking. All the other, later manuscripts have a different chapter division, each of which is shorter than those in the two early manuscripts, and they are accompanied by a rubricated title and numbering. Tesnière suggests that the creation of titles was meant not simply to clarify the movement of the narrative but to provide a prompt for the inclusion of illustrations in the text, which are the most important physical difference between the first two manuscripts and the rest of the manuscript tradition. Interestingly, in the Oxford manuscript a cursive hand dating to the late fourteenth or early fifteenth century has added in the margins the titles and numbering of the chapters taken from one of the manuscripts of the revised version – thus suggesting the overwhelming

authority that the revised versions had obtained. There is thus a dual chapter division in the Oxford manuscript, which we have reproduced in our edition.

We have attempted in our edition to maintain the readings of the Oxford manuscript (ms. *O*) whenever possible. Readings in the base manuscript that we have had to correct (and that we signal in the edition's footnotes) include: (1) passages where a word or words are missing; and (2) passages where a word or words are replaced. In the first instance, we use the abbreviation *om.* to refer to what is missing in ms. *O*, followed by the abbreviation *corr.* to indicate the siglum or sigla (mss. *G* and/or *J*) that provided the missing text; in the second instance, we indicate the word or words as found in ms. *O* and then use the abbreviation *corr.* to indicate the siglum or sigla of the control manuscripts that were used to correct the segment in ms. *O*. In the case that the two control manuscripts differ in their spelling, we use boldface type to indicate which manuscript provides the text we have used. Variants of note in the control manuscripts are also included in the footnotes.

We close with a final note regarding pagination. Pagination in medieval manuscripts is quite different from that which we are used to in printed books. Similar to the latter, the manuscript brings together leaves, predominantly made of parchment in the earliest exemplars, upon which the texts are handwritten, upon both sides. Whereas it has for centuries become the norm in printed books that each side of the printed page has a distinct numbering, in the standard pagination of manuscripts, such as the Oxford manuscript that is the base for our edition, each parchment leaf, called a folio, has the same numbering for its front side or page (*recto*) and its back side or page (*verso*). Furthermore, the copyists of early medieval manuscripts, depending upon the size of the page, tend to write the texts in columns, which make them somewhat easier to read. In the Oxford manuscript, each page has two columns, so that the description of where the text of the edition is to be found in the manuscript (should a reader want to look at the original) is based upon the number of the parchment folio, in Arabic numbers starting with 1; whether it is on the front side (r for *recto*) or the back side (v for *verso*); and which column it is in, a and b for the two on the *recto* side, and c and d for the two on the *verso* side. Thus, the opening page of the Verginia story indicates at the top left 'f. 52vd,' meaning that the text begins somewhere within the last column (d) of the back page (v) on folio number 52. The next page indicator, in the middle of the first paragraph, tells us, not surprisingly, that the last word in folio 52 is "honneste" and that the next word following it, "ordre," is at the beginning of the first column on the front side (recto) of folio 53. The beginning of each new page of the manuscript, recto and verso, is signaled in our edition by the same formula.

NOTES ON THE IMAGES

We have illustrated this volume with images drawn from various manuscripts of the *Tite-Live* and the *Roman de la rose*. One of the *Tite-Live* manuscripts is worth describing in detail, as it reveals a particular preoccupation with Verginia and Lucretia as models of female heroism.

The manuscript in question, which includes only the first decade of Livy's *Ab urbe condita*, was produced in Lille around the year 1470. The illuminations are stylistically indebted to the Wavrin Master, an artist in service to Jean de Wavrin, counselor to Philip III of Burgundy, and to the Master of Martin le Franc's *Le champion des dames* (Paris, BnF, ms. fr. 841). The manuscript seems to have been intended for a member of the Trazegnies family, as the family's motto, "Tant que vive" ("For as long as I live"), appears on the colophon. Next to the motto is the signature of a certain Arondelle, who was probably either the scribe or the illuminator.

The manuscript features thirteen pen-and-wash drawings, including a portrait of Bersuire, an image of Bersuire presenting his work to Jean le Bon (Figure 1), and eleven images illustrating events in the *Tite-Live*. Ten of the latter images accompany the stories of Lucretia and Verginia (Figures 3–12), suggesting that the manuscript may have been intended for educating noblewomen.

As far as we know, the manuscript has not been studied, though Dr. Jörn Günther Rare Books made an initial description available to us. Dr. Günther consulted two eminent manuscript experts, Dominique Vanwijnsberghe, Head of Art Historical Research and Inventory at the Royal Institute for Cultural Heritage in Brussels, and Anne D. Hedeman, Judith Harris Murphy Distinguished Professor Emerita in Art History at the University of Kansas.

The Tale of Verginia from Pierre Bersuire's *Tite-Live*

The base manuscript for this edition is Oxford, Bodleian Library, Rawlinson C 447 (*O*). Corrections have been made, and occasional variants provided, with the help of Sainte Geneviève 777 (*G*) and BnF nafr. 27401 (*J*). As we noted in the introduction, the *O* manuscript divides each book into chapters, which are in turn divided into paragraphs. The scribe typically marks chapter divisions with a slightly enlarged initial letter (usually the height of two lines) containing filigree-work, next to which, in the text or in the margin, is a rubricated capital *C* followed by the chapter number in Roman numerals, also rubricated. He marks paragraph divisions with alternating red and blue pilcrows in the text and with marginal, rubricated paragraph numbers that restart with each chapter division, though the new paragraph starting at the beginning of the chapter division is usually not indicated by a marginal "1," and numbering starts with the second paragraph. There are no titles or other forms of decoration. The *J* manuscript, the text of which is closely related to our base manuscript, by and large maintains the same chapter and paragraph divisions, including the use of similar decorated initials for chapter divisions and alternating pilcrows (including gold leaf) for paragraph divisions, but without any numbering. All of the other manuscripts, later than these two, contain a different system of shorter chapters accompanied by chapter titles and numbering, many of which coincide with the older chapter or paragraph divisions of *O* and *J*. The later chapter numbers and titles were added to the *O* manuscript as marginal notes at some point in the late fourteenth or early fifteenth century. We have preserved the dual chapter division of ms. *O* in our edition. The markings original to the *O* manuscript appear in boldface within the text. The later markings appear in italics and are set off from the text as separate paragraphs. In the older division of mss. *O* and *J*, the Verginia episode begins with par. 4 of Ch. 13 and includes the entirety of Chs. 14 and 15. In the later division, it is divided into thirteen chapters, numbered 21 to 33. Thus, the entirety of the three chapters in the early division (13–15) is in the later division, which must have become the authoritative one in the late fourteenth century, divided into thirteen chapters, numbered 21 to 33. (The later chapter 21 coincides with the beginning of the earlier chapter 13 in ms. *O*, while chapter 22, the title of which introduces the Verginia story, along with an illuminated miniature in ms. *G*, begins our edition and coincides with chapter 13, par. 4, of the older division.)

[f. 52vd]

Ci commence l'ystoire de Virginius et de Virgine sa fille et du juge Appius .xxii. [Ch. 22]

(par. 4) Un autre grant forfait fu fait en la cité qui ne termina pas a mainz honteuse fin que[1] fist jadis celluy qui, pour cause du stupre ou de corruption de Lucrece, les roys tarquiniens exilla du royaume, car non pas seulement celle meismes fin, mes encore celle meismes cause, de perdre leur empire fu aus dix homes qui avoit esté aus[2] roys. Car comme Appius Claudius fust demourez pour garder la cité, dit est, talent li prist de avoir et de corrumpre une verge du plebe[3] de qui li peres, qui avoit nom Virginius, estoit en Algide ducteur et capitain d'une honeste [f. 53ra] ordre de chevaliers, et estoit home de droiturier exemple aus champs et a l'ostel, c'est a dire en temps de guerre et en temps de pais. Et aussi sa fame et ses enfans estoient bien fourmez a l'exemple de luy. Si avoit sa fille donnee a fame[4] a un plebeyen tribunicial appellé L. Icilius, home de fier engin et experte vertu en la cause du plebe. Ceste verge donques, qui ja estoit parcreue et d'excellent biauté, avoit li dis Appius, ardans en son amour, volu atraire par dons et par prieres, mais la ou il avoit veu que toutes choses estoient en la vierge garnies de vergoingne, et de chaasté, il converti son courage a orgueilleuse et cruele violence, si commanda a un sien sergent, que l'en disoit M. Claudius, que il deist et affermast la verge estre sa serve, et que en jugement la requeist a li estre adjugiee, et que il ne sousfrist point, pour nul qui requeist, que l'en procedast en ceste chose selonc la loy des vindices.

Vindices sont les verges des sergenz que l'en metoit sur les testes de ceus qui se disoient estre franc selonc la loy, ff. de orig. jur. l. ii. C. "Cum placuisset"; laquelle loy[5] declairoit la sollemnité qui a repeter[6] liberté estoit neccessaire.[7]

(par. 5) Cestuy Claudius, regardans que le pere de la pucelle fust en l'ost, pensa que lors aroit il miex lieu de faire celle injure, si vit la vierge venir ou marchié, c'est en la place, pour ce que illueques faisoit l'en certainz jeux en

---

[1] qui *O*; corr. *GJ*
[2] au *OJ*; este roys *G*
[3] pueple *O*; corr. *GJ*
[4] d. a f. *O*; espousee *GJ*
[5] verge *O*; corr. *GJ*
[6] repeter *O*; reputer *GJ*
[7] Addition in left margin over sixteen short lines, possibly in the gothic scribal hand but in a script that is smaller and fainter.

Here begins the story of Verginius, and of his daughter Verginia, and of the judge Appius (Ch. 22)[1]

(par. 4) Another great crime was committed in the city, one that resulted in no less shameful a conclusion than did the crime that led, long ago, to the exile of the Tarquinian kings from the kingdom, on account of the rape [*stupre*] and corruption of Lucretia;[2] for not only did the same end befall the decemvirs[3] as had befallen the kings – the loss of their rule – but the cause was also the same. For it is said that when Appius Claudius remained in the city to guard it, he was seized by a desire to possess and corrupt a certain plebeian virgin,[4] whose father, named [Lucius] Verginius,[5] was in Algidum[6] as the leader and captain of an honorable company of knights.[7] He was an exemplary, law-abiding man both on the battlefield and at home – that is, in times of war and in times of peace. His wife and progeny[8] were likewise raised to follow his example. He had betrothed his daughter to a plebeian tribune named L[ucius] Icilius, a man of plucky character whose power had been proven in the cause of the plebs.[9] Said Appius, burning with love, had wished to use gifts and entreaties to seduce this virgin, who was already grown and quite beautiful; yet seeing she was protected in all things by modesty and chastity, he turned his heart to arrogant and cruel violence. Thus, he ordered one of his officers,[10] who was called M[arcus] Claudius,[11] to assert and affirm that the virgin was his slave; he was to ask the court to return her to him and was not to tolerate, no matter who might request it, that the case be judged according to the law of the vindices [*la loi des vindices*].[12]

Marginal Note: Vindices are the rods that officers placed on the heads of those who were said to be free under the law, ff. de orig. jur. l. ii. C. "Cum placuisset"; which law established the legal formality necessary to claim liberty.[13]

(par. 5) Taking note that the maiden's father was away with the army, this Claudius thought he would now have an easier opportunity to commit this wrong. He saw the virgin come to the marketplace, which is in the forum, where certain exercises were conducted in the tents used as elementary

tabernacle des letres, c'estoit la ou li enffant apprenoient; et a mis en elle[8] sa main luxurieuse et l'appella sa serve. Et li a dit estre nee serve, et li commanda qu'elle le suyst, et que s'elle ne le suyvoit, que il l'emmerroit par force, pour la quelle chose la pucelle fu esbahie. Au cri de sa norrice priant et requerant la foy des Quirites et du pueple rommain, grant assemblee y est tantost venue, qui commencierent a louer[9] et a celebrer le nom de Virginius son pere, et de Ycilius son espous, pour l'amour des quelz l'indignité de ceste chose troubla ceulz qui la connoissoient. Si la garderent lors, qu'elle ne fust esforcee. **(par. 6)** Lors a dit li demanderres que yci n'avoit point de besoing de multitude esmeue, et que il voloit aler par droit, non pas par force. Si appella la pucelle a droit, si que aveuques ceulz qui estoient present il vindrent au siege de Appius Claudius, ouquel lieu proposa li demanderres la fable dessus dite par devant Appius, qui estoit aucteur de cesti arguement. "Ceste pucelle, dist il, fu nee en ma maison, et si me fu[10] emblee & amenee a l'ostel Virginius, et a luy supposee. Et ce, dist il, je ay congneu, et pour ce je l'ay raporté a vostre jugement. Et suy prests de le prouver encore devant Virginius, a cui plus appartient de poursuyr ceste injure, se il estoit mon juge. Et dy, dist il, que ce est juste chose que entre deux elle me soit bailliee et que la chamberiere soit avant son seignour." **(par. 7)** Li advocat de la vierge alleguerent que le pere de la vierge estoit absens, a deux journees d'ilueques, pour l'estat du commun, et que il porroit venir en deux jours, qui li denonceroit, et que inique chose seroit, luy absent, contendre de la liberté de sa fille. Et pour ce requeroient que la chose fust gardee [f. 53rb] entiere jusques a la venue de luy. Et que par vertu de la loy par luy faite il requeroient[11] les vindices, selonc l'accion de liberté et que il li pleust que la vierge qui ja estoit grandeite et parcreue, ne souffrist pas avant perilz de sa rennomee que de sa liberté. Si a dit Claudius que celle loy voloit il desclairier[12] et que en celle estoit bien contenue sceure aide, se pour causes ou pour personnes ce n'estoit empeeschié. "Et a lieu celle loy quant celui qui demande liberté n'a nul autre qui y prétende avoir droit par cui la possession du demandeur peust estre occupee, la quelle chose n'est pas en cestuy cas. Et pour ce, dist il, je juge que son pere sera attendu mes que, entre deux, la pucelle sera en la garde du demandeur, et aveuques ce, il donra pleiges de la amener a droit a la venue de celui qui bien dit estre son pere." **(par. 8)** Comme il y eust plus de ceulz qui fremissoient contre l'injure de la sentence que de ceulz qui publiquement l'osassent racuser, P. Numitorius,[13] aeulz, et Ilicius, espous de la pucele, sont venu en la place. Et comme il semblast a la

---

8   elle *om. O*; corr. *G*
9   iouer *O*; corr. *GJ*
10 fu *om. O*; corr. *G*
11 requerroient *O*; corr. *G*
12 desclair *O*; corr. **GJ**
13 Munitorius *O*; corr. *J*

schools, for this is where children were educated;[14] and he placed his lustful hand on her and called her his slave.[15] He told her that she was born a slave and commanded her to follow him; he said that if she did not follow him, he would carry her off by force, which shocked the maiden. When her nurse cried out, imploring and soliciting help from the Quirites and the Roman people,[16] a great crowd soon assembled and began to praise and commend the name of Verginius, the girl's father, and that of Icilius, her groom. It was out of love for these men that the shamelessness of this situation troubled those who knew her [Verginia].[17] And so, they then protected her so that she would not be subjected to brute force [*esforcee*].[18] **(par. 6)** Then the claimant [Marcus Claudius] said that this was no place for an agitated crowd and that he wished to proceed by law, not by force. He thus summoned the maiden to appear in court, and so together with those present they went to the judicial seat of Appius Claudius.[19] Once there, the claimant presented the aforementioned lies to Appius, who was the author of the argument itself. "This maiden," he said, "was born in my house and then was stolen from me and taken to the home of Verginius and presented to him as his own. I found this out," he said, "and have therefore come to present the case to you for adjudication. I am prepared to prove my case, even if it is before Verginius himself, and even if he were to serve as judge – Verginius, for whom it would be more appropriate to prosecute this crime! I declare it is just," he said, "that in the meantime she be granted to me, that the maidservant be in the presence of her master." **(par. 7)** The virgin's advocates claimed that the virgin's father was away on state business, two days' journey away; that he could return in two days if he were notified; and that it would be unjust to stake a claim on his daughter's liberty in his absence. For this reason, they requested that the matter should remain intact until his arrival. By virtue of the law he [Appius] himself had made, they called upon the law of the vindices, in conformity with the judicial right to freedom; and so, it might please him that the virgin, who was already grown and had come of age, might not undergo threats to her reputation prior to those regarding her liberty. Then [Appius] Claudius said he wished to explain this very law, which indeed contained irrevocable support, provided it was not obstructed by juridical circumstances or persons. "For instance, this law applies when the person who claims his liberty has no one else who might profess to have the legal right that would allow them to seize possession of the claimant, which is not the case here. For this reason," he said, "I rule that the court will wait for the father but that in the meantime the maiden will be under the protection of the claimant; and in exchange, he will promise to return her to court after the return of he who claims to be her father." **(par. 8)** Since there were more of those who trembled at the injustice of the decision than of those who publicly dared to denounce it, P[ublius] Numitorius, the maiden's forebear,[20] and Icilius, her groom, came to the forum. Since it seemed to the

multitude que pour la venue d'eulz -et especialment du dit Ilicius- le licteur dist que c'estoit pour noient, et que la sentence estoit decreté, et fist reser[14] d'iluec le dit Illicius qui braioit et crioit pour ce que celle cruele injure avoit molt enflambé[15] son engin debonnaire. Si a parlé Illicius au dit Appius en ceste maniere: "De cestuy lieu, dist il, convendra il que tu me traies a fer ou a glaives. O tu Appi, qui veulz que soubz ta taisance ceste vierge soit corumpue et violee, je, dist il, l'ay espousee et l'entens a prendre vierge, non mie corrumpue. Et pour ce, dist il, tu pues appeller touz les licteurs de tes compaignons et faire venir verges et coingnies, car ceste ne demorra point dehors l'ostel de moy, Icilius. Hé, dist il, se tu as pour ce soustrait et osté au pueple romain l'aide des tribuns et provocation au peuple, qui sont les deux tours par les quelles l'en puet deffendre liberté, cuides tu que pour ce a vostre luxure soit donnee royaume et seignourie en noz enfanz et en noz fames? Forcenne toy, dist il, tant comme tu vorras en noz dos et en noz testes mais au mainz que chastee soit asseur. Et si, dist il, l'en veult faire force a ceste pucele, je, pour mon espouse, et Virginius, pour sa seule fille, requerons la loyauté des presens Quirites[16] et des chevaliers et touz homes et dieux. Et certes, dist il, Appi, pren te garde quel part tu iras, car cest cruel decret n'acompliras tu point sanz nostre[17] occision. Je te requier, Appi, derrechief et derrechief, que tu te preingnes garde que tu feras. Virginius, quant il sera venuz se preigne garde que il fera de sa fille. Mais ce sache il bien que, se il voloit [f. 53vc] donner lieu a ceste vendicacion, et laissier courre la condicion de sa fille, je la requerroie et vendiqueroie en liberté, comme m'espouse. Car certes, dist il, vie me laissera avant que foy." **(par. 9)** La multitude estoit toute esmeue, et estoit prez que noise s'envaist. Li licteur avoient avironné Icilius, mais toutes fois, oultre les menaces, il n'y ot rienz fait. Et lors a dit Appius que Icilius ne disoit pas tout ce pour deffendre la vierge, mes que ce estoit uns homs sanz repos, qui aspiroit au tribunal et qui ne requeroit autre chose mes que matiere de sedicion et de discorde, la quele il ne li donroit pas celi jour. Ainçois, afin que il sceust que ce que il faisoit, il ne faisoit pas pour cause de luxure, mais pour ce que a Virginius qui estoit absent et au nom paternal, et a liberté, il volroit aplier,[18] il ne donroit point celluy jour de sentence ne ne interposeroit point de decret. Ainçois requeroit[19] le dit Claudius et[20] voloit que quant a ce il cedast a son droit, et que il sousfrist que la vierge ne fust vendiquee ne demandee jusques au jour aprez. Et que se Virginius n'estoit present, il denunçoit desja a Iccilius et a ses[21] semblables que sa loy, c'est a dire sa convenance de faire venir Virginius dedenz deux jours, seroit a point tenue, et que constance a ce faire ne faudroit point au dyhome, et que en ce il ne useroit point des licteurs de ses compaignons, quar les siens li sousfisoient bien.

14   reser *O*; ruser *GJ*
15   enflambee *O*; corr. **GJ**
16   Quirites *om. O*; corr. **GJ**
17   moustrer *O*; corr. *GJ*
18   emploier *O*; corr. *G*
19   requerroit *O*; corr. *G*
20   et *om. OJ*; corr. *G*
21   d. des ja a yceluy et assez *O*; corr. *GJ*

crowd that it was on account of their arrival – and especially that of Icilius – that the lictor said that it was for naught, and said that the sentence had been decreed, and had Icilius pushed away from there, the aforementioned Icilius shouted and cried out, as this cruel injustice had greatly inflamed his worthy character. Then Icilius addressed himself to Appius in this manner: "You'll have to use iron or swords to get me to leave this place," he said. "Oh you, Appius, who under cover of silence wish to have this virgin corrupted and violated [*violee*],[21] know," he said, "that I have pledged to marry her and intend to take her as a virgin, not in the slightest corrupted. You can call all the lictors among your companions and have them come with rods and axes, but she will not stay anywhere else than my own home, this I, Icilius, declare. Hear this," he said, "if you have seized and taken from the Roman people the support of the tribunes and the right of appeal [*provocation*] to the people,[22] which are the two strongholds by which we defend liberty, do you really believe that on account of your lust we will grant you rule and lordship over our children and over our wives? You can come down as hard as you like on our backs and heads, but at the very least let chastity be assured. And if," he said, "anyone wishes to use force[23] against this maiden, I, on behalf of my bride, and Verginius, on behalf of his only daughter, we will both appeal to the loyalty of the Quirites present here, and of the knights, and of all men and gods. Indeed," he said, "Appius, beware what direction you are going in; for you shall not carry out this cruel decree without loss of life among us. I implore you again and again, Appius, to be careful about what you will do. Let Verginius decide what to do with his daughter when he comes. But he shall know that if he wished to allow this request for power [on the part of Marcus Claudius] to subsist and allow the social status of his daughter to be taken away, I would ask for her hand in marriage and secure her liberty as my wife. For surely," he said, "I will lose my life before my good faith."[24] **(par. 9)** The crowd was greatly moved and was on the verge of breaking into conflict. The lictors had surrounded Icilius, but nonetheless, beyond making threats, nothing happened. Then, Appius declared that Icilius was not saying all this to defend the virgin; rather, he was an unsettled man who aspired to the tribunate and who sought nothing other than a pretext for sedition and discord, which he [Appius] would not grant him that day. Instead, so that Icilius would know that Appius was doing what he was doing not out of lust but because he would like to do service to Verginius, who was absent, to the state of fatherhood, and to freedom, he [Appius] would not in the slightest pronounce any sentence that day nor would he enact any decree. Instead, he would ask said [Marcus] Claudius to waive his right and accept that the virgin would neither be claimed nor pursued until the following day. He made it known to Icilius and his ilk that if Verginius was not present then, his ruling, which required Verginius to return within two days, would be enforced punctually. The decemvir would not be lacking in firmness, and he would not use his friends' lictors, for his own would easily suffice.

*Comment Icilius espoux de Virgine envoia querre Virginius son pere. xxiii
[Ch. 23]*

(par. 10)[22] Comme donques le temps de ceste injure fust differé et li advocat
de la pucelle s'en fussent allé, il envoierent tantost le frere de Icilius et le fil
du dit Numitor, qui estoient tres apert jouvencel, a l'ost pour querre le dit
Virginius et li dire que tout le salut de la pucelle dependoit de luy, se il pouoit
le jour assigné estre presens en jugement. Si coururent la li duy jouvencel a
chevaux abrievez et porterent au pere le message. Entre deux li demanderres
dessus diz demandoit la pucelle et si offroit a donner pleiges. Et aussi faisoit
Icilius tout au contraire en parloingnant et en passant le temps diligemment,
si que toute la multitude ouy que li messaige aloient en l'ost, leverent leurs
mainz, et dist chascuns que il estoit prest a plegier pour la fille affin que elle
demourast en la garde de Icilius, qui en plourant leur rendi merciz et leur
a dit que le jour ensuyant il useroit de leur courtoisie. Et ainsi fu receue la
damoiselle par le plegage de ses amis. **(par. 11)** Aprez ce que toutes autres
causes pour la cure de ceste estoient dellaissiees, Appius, qui avoit attendu
grant piece pour ce que il ne[23] feust veus soy estre assiz ou venus en jugement
pour ceste besoingne, veu que nul ne venoit plus en jugement, s'en alla a
son hostel, et a escript a ses compaingnons qui gouvernoient l'ost que ilz ne
donnassent point de licence [f. 53vd] ne de conduit a Virginius de retourner,
mes ainçois le meissent em prison. Mais son malvais conseil, si comme drois
estoit, fu un petit trop tart, car Virginius prist son congié et s'en estoit desja
tres bien matin partiz avant le jour. Et ainsi les letres pour luy retenir furent
pour noient donnees et rendues.

*Comment Virginius vint en jugement avec Virgine sa fille. Et comment Appius
donna sentence contre la pucelle .xxiiii. [Ch. 24]*

(par. 12) Ainsi fu dont que le jour assigné tres bien matin Virginius comme
toute la cité fust venue ou marchié. Attendans la besoingne vint ou marchié en
robe de duel ville et honnie, et sa fille ensement, laquelle il admena aveuques
soy en la compaingnie de plusieurs matrones. A grant assemblee de pueple si
se prist a aler entour les ordres et a prier les hommes et a demander l'aide[24] de
chascun, non pas par grace comme pour dieu en recordant comment il avoit
tant de fois esté en la bataille pour leurs fames et pour leurs enfans, et que il

---

22   There is no marginal indicator for par. 10 in *O*, though there is a blue pilcrow in the
text.
23   ne *om. O*; corr. *GJ*
24   lordre *O*; corr. **GJ**

How Icilius, Verginia's groom, sent for Verginius, her father (Ch. 23)

(par. 10) Since the crime had thus been put off for a time and the advocates of the maiden had gone off by themselves, they immediately sent Icilius's brother and said Numitorius's son, who were both active young men, to the army to find said Verginius and tell him that the maiden's very salvation depended on him and his ability to appear in court on the appointed day. The two young men made haste to get there on speedy horses and carried the message to the father. In the meantime, the aforementioned claimant [Marcus Claudius] petitioned for the maiden and accordingly offered to provide sureties.[25] So also did Icilius, acting entirely in opposition by delaying and tactically wasting time, such that the whole crowd heard that the messengers were headed to the army. They raised up their hands, and each man said he was prepared to furnish sureties for the girl so she might remain under the protection of Icilius. In tears, Icilius offered them his thanks and told them that the following day he would avail himself of their generosity. Thus, the maiden was received by him thanks to the sureties of her friends. **(par. 11)** After all the other cases had been dropped for the sake of this one, Appius – who had waited a long time so that no one would notice that he had come to court and sat in judgment for this matter alone, and given that no one else was coming in to present a case – went to his home and wrote to his friends who were commanders in the army. He asked that they refuse to offer Verginius leave or safe-conduct but rather that they throw him in prison. Yet his evil counsel was a bit too late, as was just; for Verginius took his leave early in the morning and was already gone by sunrise. Thus, the letter meant to detain him was sent and delivered in vain.

How Verginius came to court with his daughter Verginia. And how Appius pronounced a sentence against the maiden (Ch. 24)

(par. 12) Thus it was that on the appointed day, rather early in the morning, Verginius, along with the entire city, came to the marketplace. In expectation of the trial, he came to the marketplace in sordid and soiled mourning dress with his daughter dressed much the same;[26] and he led her forth in the company of numerous matrons. With a large group of people assembled, he then began to circulate among the ranks, imploring the men and asking for help from each one. He did not plead for grace, as one would of a god; rather, he recalled how many times he had gone to battle for their wives and for their children, and

n'y avoit nul de cui l'en peust recorder plus de beaux, fiers, et chevalereux fais en batailles que de li. "Mais, disoit il, que nous pourfiteroit il se il convenoit soustenir a noz enfans, la cité estant paisible, les derreniers maulz que l'en craint quant les citez sont prises, c'est a dire, servitude et luxure?" Ces choses s'en aloit Virginius tout entour criant et aussi comme preeschant. Et Icilius de l'autre part faisoit semblablement et la compaingnie des fames esmouvoit plus chascun par son taisible pleur que ne faisoit nulle autre vois. **(par. 13)** Si grant force de desverie, non pas d'amour, avoit troublé le courage de Appius que luy contre toutes ces choses perseverans a obstiné courage s'en monta en son siege. Et comme le demandeur se plainsist de ce que par grant orgueil ceulz de la partie adverse n'avoient onques avant le jour daignié parler a luy de ceste besoingne avant que il venist pour demander et Virginius pour respondre, li dis Appius donna sentence contre la pucele. Et ja soit ce que je ne truisse point de quelles paroles il usa en si vilain decret, toutesvoies cuide je que il iuga contre les vindices selonc servitude. C'est a dire que il la juga a estre vendiquee et occupee comme serve. **(par. 14)** Premierement granz esbahissemens pour l'admiration de si cruel decret a touz fait arrester et puis par aucun poy de temps ont tuit tenu silence. Et aprez ce, comme M. Claudius, avironnéz de matrones, alast pour prandre la vierge et le plour lamentans des dames se fust mis au devant, Virginius leva ses mainz contre le dit Appius, et a dit ces paroles: "Appi, dist il, je n'ay pas espousé ma fille et si l'ay norrie pour la donner aus noces, nun pas au bordel, et nientmainz il te plaist a guise de brebis et de bestes sauvages toy esbrivier es delis de la char. Je ne say mie se ceulz cy le sousterront; je croy que non mie ceulz qui avront armes." **(par. 15)** Comme li demanderres fust rapellez [f. 54ra] par la compaingnie des dames et des advocaz de la pucele, li diz homs Appius, aliené son courage a luxure, disoit que non pas seulement par l'injure que Icilius fist hier ne par la violence que Virginius fist huy, mes encores par autres certainnes demonstrances, il avoit compris et esprouvé que toute celle nuit il avoient fait couvens et assemblees par mi la cité a esmouvoir sedicion. Et pour ce que il n'estoit pas ignorans de leurs emprises, il estoit descenduz illueques aveuques genz armez, non pas pour violer nulle personne paisible, mais afin de contraindre[25] ceulz qui troublent le repos et la pais de la cité, et si comme il appartient a la magesté de son empire. Et pour ce dist il qu'il vaulroit mieulz que l'en se tenist coy. "Toutesvoies, dist il, tu licteur, fay ruser celle tourbe, et donne voie au seigneur de prendre sa mancipe ou sa serve." **(par. 16)** Et comme Appius, plainz d'ire, eust ces choses hautement dites, la multitude se rusa tout par soy et la pucele demoura toute seule, comme proie deguerpie et exposee a injure.

---

[25]   cohercier *JG*

how there was none among them who could recall more excellent, proud, and chivalric deeds in battle than his. "Yet," he said, "what good would it do us if, while the city is at peace, our children must put up with the worst ills one fears when cities are seized, in other words slavery and lust?" Verginius went all around calling out these things, almost as if he were preaching. Icilius did much the same on the other side [of the marketplace]; and the company of women, with its silent weeping, moved everyone more than any other voice could. **(par. 13)** A great force of madness, rather than love, had agitated the heart of Appius such that he hardened his heart against all these things and mounted his judicial seat. Inasmuch as the claimant was complaining that those of the opposing party had, in their great arrogance, never before this day deigned to speak with him about this affair, that is, before he came to present his case and Verginius came to respond, said Appius pronounced his sentence against the maiden. Though I would be hard pressed to find what words he used in so despicable a decree, I nonetheless believe that he ruled against the vindices and in favor of slavery. In other words, he ruled that the maiden would be given as property and seized as a slave. **(par. 14)** At first, everyone stopped dead because of their great astonishment, shocked at so cruel a decree; and then for some short amount of time, they all kept silent. Afterward, as M[arcus] Claudius, surrounded by matrons, went to claim the virgin, and as the ladies broke out in plaintive weeping, Verginius raised up his hands toward said Appius and uttered these words: "Appius," he said, "I did not betroth my daughter [to you]; and I raised her to be given in marriage, not to the brothel; and yet you have seen fit to imitate livestock and wild animals by throwing yourself into the crimes of the flesh. I have no idea whether these men here will support it; I believe the ones who bear arms will not at all." **(par. 15)** As the claimant was being pushed back by the company of ladies and the advocates of the maiden, the decemvir Appius, his heart crazed by lust, said that not only because of the insults Icilius made yesterday, not only because of the violence Verginius did that same day, but also because of other certain signs, he had understood and established that all night long they had gathered and assembled throughout the city to promote sedition. Since he was not ignorant of their undertakings, he had come there with men-at-arms, not to injure any peaceful person but to impede those who trouble the stability and peace of the city; and this was as befits the majesty of his rule. For this reason, he said that it would be best if everyone would remain calm. "Nonetheless," he said, "you, lictor, push back this mob and make room for the lord to take his servant or his slave." **(par. 16)** As Appius, filled with rage, said these things in a loud voice, the crowd pulled back of their own accord, and the maiden was left all alone, like a prey abandoned and exposed to an injustice.

Comment Virginius occist Virgine sa fille .xxv. [Ch. 25]

Et lors Virginius, la ou il vit que il n'y avoit nul remede, se prist a parler en dissimulacion aveuques Appius debonnairement et a dit ces paroles: "Appi, dist il, je te pri au commencement que tu pardonnes a la doleur paternal se je ay contre toy nulles choses dites et inveheez[26] mainz debonnairement, et te pri que tu me sueffres que je puisse ci demander devant la pucelle a sa norrice, secretement, quele cause ce puet estre, affin que, se je ay esté faulsement reputez son pere, je m'en departe a plus lié courage."[27] Si le li ottroya Appius. Et lors Virginius prist la fille et la norrice et les trait a part delez celi lieu que l'en appelloit les tavernes cloacines. Et illueques prist un coutel albanien et a dit ces paroles: "O tu, dist il, ma fille, en ceste seule maniere que je te puis vendiquier et garder en liberté, je t'i vendique et aveue." Et lors a fichié le coutel par mi le piz de[28] la vierge, et regardanz a la chaiere[29] de Appius a dit ces paroles: "O tu Appi, dist il, je te consacre, toy et ton chief,[30] en cestui vierge sanc." Et lors se sourdi grant clamour a si cruel forfait, et s'est levez Appius, et commanda prandre Virginius, mais quelque part que il aloit il se faisoit voie aveuques son glaive. Et aussi la multitude de ceulz qui le suioient le deffandoit jusqu'atant que il vint a la porte. **(par. 17)** Icilius et Numitorius pristrent le corps sanz sanc. Et l'emporterent en demonstrant au pueple l'outrage de Appius et la fourme maleuree de la pucele et plouroient la neccessité du pere, et les matrones les suyvoient en lamentant et en demandant se ce estoit la condicion de procreer et se ce estoient les salaires de garder chasteté. Et adjoustoient les dames autres plainz et paroles qui [f. 54rb] de tant estoient plus piteuses et miserables comme doleur feminine[31] a plus triste et a plus feible courage les scet plus agrever; et aussi la vois de touz les homes, et especialment du dit Icilius estoit plainne des indignations publiques, et especialment de puissance tribunicial et de la provocation au pueple getees de la ville. Si que toute la multitude fu esmeue, partie pour la cruauté du forfait, partie pour l'esperance que chascuns avoit lors pour occasion de ces choses de recouvrer liberté.

---

26   parlees *O*; corr. *GJ*
27   lie le c. *O*; corr. *G*
28   le piz de *om. O*; corr. **GJ**
29   chiere *O*; corr. *G*
30   ceph *O*; corr. *G*
31   famine *OG*; corr. *J*

How Verginius killed Verginia, his daughter (Ch. 25)

Then Verginius, seeing there was no remedy to be had, began to speak courteously to Appius, albeit deceptively; and he said these words: "Appius," he said, "I first pray that you grant pardon to paternal grief, if I have uttered and spoken certain things against you less than gracefully; and I pray you to allow me to privately interrogate, here in the presence of the maiden, her nurse to find out what might be at the root of this affair, such that, if I have falsely been considered her father, I may leave here with a lighter heart." Appius granted this to him. Then, Verginius took his daughter and the nurse and led them aside, near that place called the cloacinal huts.[27] He then took out an Albanian knife[28] and spoke these words: "Oh you, my daughter" he said, "since it is in this manner alone that I may protect you and maintain your freedom, I thus reclaim you with it and recognize you as my own."[29] Then he plunged the knife directly into the virgin's breast and, looking toward Appius's judicial seat, spoke these words: "Oh you, Appius," he said, "I execrate you [*je te consacre*], you and your life,[30] with this virgin blood." A great clamor then sprung up at so cruel a crime, and Appius stood up and ordered that Verginius be seized; yet wherever he went, he made a path for himself with his sword. Also, the crowd of those who followed him defended him until he reached the gate. **(par. 17)** Icilius and Numitorius took the lifeless body; and they carried it off, displaying to the people Appius's transgression and the maiden's unfortunate appearance. They wept over the father's necessity, and the matrons followed them, lamenting and asking whether this was the nature of producing children and if these were the rewards for protecting chastity. The ladies added other plaints and speeches, which were even more piteous and miserable, inasmuch as feminine grief, with its sadder and weaker heart, knows better how to devastate them. At the same time, the collective voice of all the men, and especially that of said Icilius, was filled with the indignations felt by all people, especially regarding tribunician power and the right of appeal to the people, which had been tossed out of the city. This happened in such a way that the entire crowd was agitated, in part inspired by the cruelty of the offense, in part by the hope everyone now held for recovering liberty on account of these things."

Comment Appius commanda a prendre Iccilius, l'espoux Virgine, et comment le pueple le deffendi .xxvi. [Ch. 26]

(.C. xiiii [Ch. 14]) (par. 1)[32] Appius, la ou il vit que le pueple fu si fort esmeus, a commandé a appeller Icilius et que l'en le preist et amenast se il n'y voloit venir. Et a la parfin, comme la tourbe ne daingnast faire voie a ses appariteurs, luy meismes a grant tourbe de jouvenciaux patriciens s'est boutez en la presse, et a commandé que Ilicius fust mis en liens. Mais entour Illicius estoit non pas seulement la multitude, mais en oultre li prince de la multitude L. Valerius et M. Oracius, li quel ruserent le licteur, et li distrent que se il voloit aler par droit et entendre raison, Ycilius se voloit vendiquier et soustraire du pouoir Appius, qui estoit personne privee; et que se par force il le voloit prendre, il li monsterroient que illueques il estoient aussi fors comme luy. Si envay li licteurs du dy homme Valere et Orace, mais la multitude a brisiees ses fasces.[33] Et lors Appius s'en monta en hault pour concionner et Valeres et Oraces l'ont suy, les quelz, quant il parloient en concion, la multitude l'ooit paisiblement. Et quant Appius concionnoit il siffloient et trepoient que il ne fust oys, si que Valeres commandoit aus licteurs que pour le bien de l'Empire Romain il se departissent de cestui privé[34] et ne li feissent obseque ne servise. **(par. 2)** Lors Appius, brisiez ses couragez[35] pour doubte de la mort, s'en[36] entra coiement, au non-sceu[37] de ses adversaires, la teste couverte, en la prouchainne maison du marchié; et Spurius Oppius, pour faire aide a son compaignon, s'en est entrez ou marchié d'autre part. Et voians leur empire par force vaincu, heüs plusieurs conseilz, et consentanz aus uns et aus autres, commença a avoir paour si que en la parfin il commanda a assembler le senat, lequel apaisa la multitude pour ce que il veoient que les fais des dis homes par la plus grant partie desplaisoient aus pers et esperoient que par le senat porroit estre fenie leur dure puissance. **(par. 3)** Li senas ordena que l'en ne escharnesist[38] pas le plebe,[39] mais que seur toutes choses faisoit il a pourveoir que la venue de Virginius ne feist[40] en l'ost nulz esmouvemens. Si ont esté envoié des plus jones des pers en l'ost, qui lors estoit logiez ou Mont de Vecillye et denoncierent aus [f. 54vc] diz homes que en toutes guises il gardassent les chevaliers de sedicion et d'esmouvement.

---

[32] As is usual in ms. *O*, the scribe does not indicate the first paragraph with a rubricated number in the margin at the beginning of a new chapter, as he does for all other numbered paragraphs. For the sake of clarity, we have added this marking. See our headnote above.

[33] falses *O*; corr. ***GJ***

[34] lieu prive *O*; corr. *GJ*

[35] brisa son courage *O*; corr. *GJ*

[36] et sen *O*; corr. *GJ*

[37] a deceu ***GJ***

[38] irritast *GJ*

[39] pueple *O*; corr. *GJ*

[40] fust *OJ*; corr. *G*

How Appius ordered Icilius, Verginia's groom, be seized; and how the people defended him (Ch. 26)

(Ch. 14) (par. 1) Seeing that the people there were so strongly agitated, Appius commanded that Icilius be summoned and seized, and that he be brought forward if he did not wish to come. In the end, as the mob did not deign to make a path for his officers, he thrust himself into the crush with a great mob of young patrician[31] men and ordered that Icilius be put in fetters. Yet all around Icilius was not just the crowd but also the leaders of the crowd, L[ucius] Valerius and M[arcus] Horatius,[32] who pushed the lictor back and said to him that if he, the lictor, wanted to proceed by law and take account of reason,[33] Icilius wished to liberate [*vendiquier*] and withdraw himself from the power of Appius,[34] who was an ordinary citizen;[35] but that if he wanted to take him by force, they would show him in that place that they were as strong as he.[36] The decemvir's lictor then attacked Valerius and Horatius, but the crowd broke his fasces.[37] Then, Appius raised himself up to deliver a harangue, and Valerius and Horatius followed him. When these two uttered their harangue, the crowd listened to them quietly. But when Appius uttered his, they whistled and made a racket so that he might not be heard. As a result, Valerius commanded the lictors that for the good of the Roman Empire they take their leave of this private individual and neither offer him obedience nor pay him homage. **(par. 2)** Then Appius, his spirit broken out of fear of death, stealthily entered the house nearest to the marketplace, unbeknownst to his adversaries and with his head covered; and Spurius Oppius[38] entered the marketplace from the other side to offer aid to his companion. Seeing their rule defeated by force, having received many suggestions, and agreeing with one after the other, he became fearful, such that in the end he ordered that the Senate be assembled. This action appeased the crowd, because they saw that the deeds of the decemvirs displeased the greater part of the patricians and hoped that with the involvement of the Senate their harsh power could be put to an end. **(par. 3)** The Senate ordered that no one provoke the plebs, but that above all things, it was necessary to ensure that the arrival of Verginius would not cause any uprisings among the army. Some of the youngest patricians were sent to the army, which was stationed then at Mount Vecilius;[39] and they proclaimed to the decemvirs that in every way possible they keep the knights from sedition and uprising.

*Comment Virginius vint en l'ost et prononça le fait de sa fille Virgine, et
comment l'ost s'en vint a Rome .xxvii. [Ch. 27]*

(par. 4)[41] La ou Virginius vint es tentes il y a tantost esveillié plus grant bruyt
que il n'avoit laissié en la cité. Car oultre ce que il vint acompaingniez de
quatre cenz homes qui enflamméz s'estoient pour cause de l'indignité de la
chose, si s'estoient mis en voie aveuques luy, la ou l'en le vit le glaive ou
poing et couvert de sanc, il converti en soy touz ceulz de l'ost. Et aussi la
multitude des togues veues es tentes faisoient sembler celle multitude estre
plus grande que elle n'estoit. Si demanderent li chevalier a Virginius que ce
estoit, et au premier il se prist a plourer et fu grant piece sanz ce que il peust
parler. Et a la parfin, la ou, par la venue de ceulz qui y acoururent, la tourbe se
assembla et silence fu faite, il leur exposa tout par ordre toutes les choses
faites. Et aprez ce il, tendans et joingnans ses mainz, prioit ses compaingnons
chevaliers que ce qui estoit le forfait de Appius Claudius il ne voulsissent pas
atribuer a li et que il ne li voulsissent pas contrester ne nuire comme a murdrier
et a patricide de ses enfans. Et alleguoit que la vie de sa fille li estoit trop plus
chiere que la mort, se elle eust peu franche et chaste vivre, mais que comme il
la veist comme serve ravir a stupre et a ribauderie, il li sembla que mielx estoit
perdre ses enfans par mort que par honteuse vie. Et disoit en oultre que
misericorde l'avoit fait[42] cheoir en semblance de cruauté, et que il n'eust point
demouré vis aprez sa vie, se il n'eust eu esperance de vengier sa mort a l'aide
de ses compaingnons chevaliers. Et leur disoit encore que il avoient femmes,
suers, et filles et que la ribauderie de Appius n'estoit pas estainte aveuques sa
fille, mais que de tant comme elle sera de ceci plus non-punie, de tant sera elle
plus esfrenee. Et que fortune en autruy calamité et misere[43] leur avoit donné
tres bel enseignement de eschiver semblable injure. Et que quant a soy estoit
il de ce asseur, car sa fame, ce disoit il, estoit delivre de ce peril par sa destinee,
pour ce qu'elle estoit ou vielle ou laide, et sa fille en estoit delivre par dolente,
mais par honneste, mort, pour ce que elle ne pouoit plus vivre chaaste et que
en son hostel n'avoit plus point de lieu a la ribauderie Appius, et que[44] d'autre
violence, se il la li fait, delivra il son corps o tel courage comme il a delivré le
corps de sa fille, et chascun des autres meitte conseil en soy, et en ses enfans,
se il veult. **(par. 5)** Quant Virginius ot crié ces choses, la multitude li a dit a
haute vois que elle ne faudra point a sa doleur, ne a leur liberté. Et aussi li
togue, qui aveuques lui estoient venu merlé en la tourbe des chevaliers en eulz
plaingnant et en enseignant comme a Romme ooit on et veoit tant de choses

----

[41]   There is no marginal indicator for par. 4 in *O*, though there is a red pilcrow in the
text.
[42]   fait *om. O*; corr. *G*
[43]   nuisance **G***J*
[44]   q. pour paour d'autre *G*

How Verginius reached the army and announced what happened to his daughter Verginia, and how the army returned to Rome (Ch. 27)

(**par. 4**) When Verginius came to the encampment,[40] he immediately aroused there an even greater tumult than he had left behind in the city. For beyond the fact that he came accompanied by four hundred men, who were outraged at the disgracefulness of the affair and had joined him on his journey, when all those in the army saw him with sword in hand and covered in blood, he arrested their attention. Also, the multitude of togas seen in the encampment made this crowd appear larger than it was.[41] The knights asked Verginius what this was about, and at first, he began to weep; for a long time, he was incapable of speaking. In the end, when, with the arrival of all those who rushed there, the throng assembled and fell silent, he recounted to them in an orderly fashion all the things that had been done. Afterward, stretching out his hands and joining them together, he implored his comrade knights that they refuse to attribute to him that which was the crime of Appius Claudius and that they refuse to stand against him or harm him as if he were a murderer and a parricide of his own progeny. He pleaded that his daughter's life was far dearer to him than death, if she could have lived free and chaste; but that as he saw her being abducted as a slave to defilement[42] and debauchery, it seemed to him that it was better to lose his progeny to death than to a shameful life. He said in addition that compassion had caused him to fall into a semblance of cruelty, and that he would not have remained alive at all after her life [was ended] if he had not had hope of avenging her death with the help of his comrade knights. He further told them that they had wives, sisters, and daughters; that Appius's debauchery was not extinguished along with his daughter; and that the longer it went unpunished, that much more would it be unbridled. Fortune had given them in the calamity and misery of another a very fine lesson on how to evade similar injury. He added that, as for him, he felt secure on this count: for his wife was free from this danger by her destiny, as she was either old or ugly; his daughter was freed from it by a mournful, but honorable, death; that there was no longer any place in his home for Appius's debauchery; and that as for other violence, if [Appius] does any to him, he will defend his person with the same courage as he defended his daughter's person, and each of the others should find his own remedy, for him and for his children, as he wishes. (**par. 5**) When Verginius had shouted out these things, the crowd told him at full voice that it would certainly not fail in its obligation to his sorrow, nor to their own liberty. Also, the citizens [*li togue*] who had come with him, and who mixed into the throng of knights, complaining to them, and explaining how in Rome one heard and saw so many outrageous things, made known to

indignes, monstroient a chascun comment toutes choses estoient a Romme [f. 54vd] troublees et desolees. Si vindrent aprez eulz aucun qui disoient que a poy que Appius ne avoit esté tuez, et qu'il s'en estoit allez en exil. Ces paroles contraindrent chascun a crier "aus armes" et que l'en queullist ses banieres, et que l'en s'en allast a Romme. Et li dy homme, qui estoient troublé pour les choses que il veoient ensembleement aveuques celles que il ooient, coururent li uns de ça, li autres de la, parmi les tentes pour apaisier les esmouvemens des chevaliers.[45] Et ja soit ce que il ouvrassent lors molt doucement, nientmainz l'en ne leur donnoit nulle response, mais ce disoient bien li chevalier que, qui les vouldroit empeeschier, il li monsterroient que il estoient armé et que il estoient homme. (par. 6) Ces choses demenees ainsi, il s'en allerent touz ensemble a Rome et s'en alerent asseoir ou Mont Aventin. Et ainsi comme le plebe[46] leur venoit a l'encontre, chascun les admonnestoit a repeter liberté et a creer tribuns, et nulle autre vois ou violence vous n'oyssiez en eulz. Et lors Spurius Appius adjousta le senat, et ne li plaisoit pas que l'en feist nulle chose asprement contre le plebe,[47] mesmement comme li dy home eussent esté cause de la sedicion, si leur a l'en envoié trois legas, homes consulaires. Ce furent Sp. Tarpenius, G. Julius, P. Sulpicius, qui de par le senat leur demandassent de cuy commandement il avoient lessié leurs tentes, ou que il demandoient, eulz qui avoient assis le Mont Aventin, ou comment ce estoit que il avoient laissié la guerre des anemis et eussent pris leur pays. (par. 7) A ces choses ne failloit pas response, mes seulement qui la response donnast, comme il n'eussent nul certain capitain et chascun par soy ne se osast offrir a celle envie, mes toutesvoies a la multitude crié et dit que l'en leur envoiast L. Valerium et M. Oracium et que a ceulz il donnassent response. Et laissiez les legas, li dis Virginius[48] admonnestoit les cheualiers et leur disoit que l'en avoit doubte en chose non pas trop grant pour ce que la multitude estoit sanz chief; toutesvoies avoit on donné response non pas inutile, plus par fortune que par commun assentement, et que il conseilloit que l'en creast dix tribuns qui ordonnassent de la chose publique et que pour honeur de chevalerie il feussent appellé tribun de chevaliers. Et comme cesti honneur fust defferé tout premierement au dit Virginius, il leur dit ces paroles: "Seigneurs, dist il, je vous prie que ces jugemens et ces opinions que vous avez de moy vous reservez et otroiez a ceulz qui sont meilleurs pour voz besoingnes et pour les moies. Car certes, dist il, ma fille que je avoie seule ne me porroit sousfrir nulle honneur estre ad present agreable; et aussi ne seroit pas vostre pourfit que en chose si troublee, ceulz soient voz souverainz qui sont prochainz a hayne et a envie. Car se l'en a de moy besoing, aussi bien me porra l'en prendre [f. 55ra] tout privé, comme se j'estoie en office publique." Si furent lors créé dix tribuns de cheualiers.

---

[45] The scribe here repeated "et eulz apaisier" and then deleted it with underlined dots.
[46] pueple *O*; corr. *GJ*
[47] peuple *O*; corr. *GJ*
[48] Vignilus *O*; corr. *GJ*

everyone that everything in Rome was disturbed and destroyed. After them came some who said that Appius had nearly been killed and that he had gone off into exile. These words led everyone to call "to arms" and to gather up the standards and head off to Rome. The decemvirs, who were disturbed by the things they saw along with those they heard,[43] ran through the encampment, one this way, another that, to appease the knights' uprisings. Even though they worked rather gently, nonetheless no one gave them any response; but this the knights did indeed say, that whoever wished to obstruct them, they would show him that they were armed and that they were men.[44] **(par. 6)** These things having been conducted in this way, they all went off together to Rome and went to occupy the Aventine Hill.[45] As the plebs came to meet them, each man exhorted them to claim liberty and to elect tribunes, and you would have heard no other expression of advice or aggression among them. Then, Spurius Appius [Oppius][46] assembled the Senate, which was unwilling to allow anyone to do anything harsh against the plebs, especially as the decemvirs had been the cause of the sedition. They [the Senators] sent to them [the knights] three legates, principal magistrates. These were Sp[urius] Tarpenius [Tarpeius], G[aius] Julius, and P[ublius] Sulpicius,[47] who were supposed to ask them on behalf of the Senate by whose command they had abandoned their encampment; or what they were demanding, they who had occupied the Aventine Hill; or how it was that they had abandoned the war against the enemies and had taken over their own country. **(par. 7)** A response to these things was not lacking, but only someone who might give the response, as they [the knights] had no definite leader and each man on his own did not dare expose himself to invidious treatment; but nonetheless the crowd cried out and said that they should send them L[ucius] Valerius and M[arcus] Horatius and that they would give them a response. The legates having left, said Verginius admonished the knights and said to them that they were in a state of uncertainty regarding a matter of no great importance because the crowd was without a leader; nonetheless, they had given an answer that was not useless, though it was more by luck than by common accord; and he advised them to elect ten tribunes who would organize the common estate[48] and who, in honor of knighthood, should be called tribunes of the knights.[49] As this honor was initially conferred upon said Verginius, he spoke these words to them: "Lords," he said, "I implore that you set aside these judgments and opinions you have of me and grant them to those who are better suited to your needs and to mine. For surely," he said, "the daughter I had, the only one,[50] could not allow me to find any honor agreeable at present; also, it would not be to your advantage in so troubled a situation for those who are a close target of hatred and enmity to be your rulers. For indeed, if my help is needed, it will be as easily gotten from me, a private citizen, as it would be if I were in public office." Ten tribunes of the knights were then elected.

(par. 8) Li os qui estoit en Sabins d'autre partie ne fu pas en repos, car illueques, aucteurs a ce, Ycile et Numitor, cecession et departance des dix hommes fu faite, et la memoire de la mort Siccius fu renouvelee, non pas par menour mouvement de courage que la nouvele fame de la vierge, si honteusement a luxure requise, les avoit esmeus. Et lors la ou Yciles oy[49] que l'en avoit créé en Adventin tribun des cheualiers, affin que la prerogative des comices des tribuns des chevaliers, qui aussi faisoient a creer en celi ost, ne fust pas faite aprez les comitez des tribuns plebeyenz, luy, comme savans des choses populaires et comme home de puissance, mist diligence que, avant que l'en allast en la cité, il creassent de semblable pouoir celi meismes nombre de tribuns; la quelle chose faite, il s'en entrerent en la cité par la porte Colline et soubz leurs banieres, par leurs compaingnies, il s'en alerent jusques en Adventin et illueques, conjoint a l'autre ost, il baillierent aus vint tribuns trestout plenier pouoir que il creassent deux de leur compangnie qui ordonnassent de la somme des choses, si creerent M. Oppium et Sextum Manlium. **(par. 9)** Li per curieux de l'estat du commun, comme il heussent chascun jour senat, gastoient leur temps plus en tençons que en conseilz. La mort de Siccius et la ribauderie de Appius et les choses malfaites en chevalerie estoient obicees aus dix homes, et plaisoit a touz que Valeres et Oraces allassent en Aventin parler au plebe[50] et il disoient que il n'iroient point se les dix hommes avant tout euvre ne se demetoient de leur magistrat, du quel il estoient privé passé avoit un an, et li dy home devoient retorner a l'ordre des privez et a l'estat des autres pers; et disoient que l'estat publique ne laisseroient il pas jusques atant que les loys pour les queles establir il estoient créé fussent toutes parfaites. Pour les quelles choses, comme li plebes[51] feust certifiez par Duillius, qui avoit esté tribuns du plebe,[52] car[53] l'en ne proufiteroit[54] riens, tant avoit il de dissencions entre les pers, li plebes,[55] par conseil de li, se parti de Adventin et s'en ala en la Montaingne Sainte. Et leur disoit li diz Duilius que li per, jusques atant que il veissent la cité deguerpir, ne metroient en ces choses cure ne diligence; et que la Sainte Montaingne leur feroit recorder de la constance du plebe,[56] et que les choses ne se porroient retourner a concorde, se le pouoir du plebe[57] n'estoit premierement restitué, c'est a dire de creer tribuns et de provocation.

---

49 oy *om. OJ*; corr. *G*
50 pueple *O*; corr. *GJ*
51 pueples *O*; corr. **G***J*
52 pueple *O*; corr. *GJ*
53 que *G*
54 pourfitoit *O*; corr. *G*
55 pueples *O*; corr. *GJ*
56 pueple *O*; corr. *GJ*
57 pueple *O*; corr. *GJ*

(par. 8) Elsewhere, the army that was among the Sabines was not at rest;[51] for there, with Icilius and Numitorius as leaders, secession and separation from the decemvirs were accomplished, and the memory of the death of Siccius was revived,[52] not that the movement of feeling provoked by the recent renown of the virgin, so shamefully pursued out of lust, had diminished.[53] Then, when Icilius, who heard that they had elected a tribune of the knights at the Aventine, in order that the prior vote in the *comitium*[54] of the tribunes of the knights, which ought to be elected among this army as well, should not be cast after the comitia of the plebeian tribunes, he, as a man of power who knew about popular affairs, took steps so that, before they should come to the city, they would elect with similar authority the exact same number of tribunes; this thing having been done, they entered into the city through the Colline Gate;[55] and under their banners, among their companies, they went as far as the Aventine and there, joined to the other army, they granted an entirely unrestricted power to the twenty tribunes so that they might elect two from their company who would command from on high; and so, they elected M[arcus] Oppius and Sextus Manilius.[56] (par. 9) Anxious about the common estate, the senators [*li per*] convened the Senate every day but wasted their time with more quarrels than deliberations. The death of Siccius and the debauchery of Appius and the knights' shameful behavior in the field were laid at the feet of the decemvirs, and all agreed that Valerius and Horatius ought to go to the Aventine to speak to the plebs. They [Valerius and Horatius] said that they would not go at all unless the decemvirs, before taking any other action, should renounce their magistracy, from which they were discharged more than a year before; and that the decemvirs ought to return to the order of private citizens and to the estate of the other patricians.[57] They [the decemvirs] said that they would not leave public office until the moment when the laws they were elected to establish had been entirely fulfilled.[58] Because of these things, as the plebs were assured by [Marcus] Duillius,[59] who had been a tribune of the plebs, that they would make no progress in anything, so great was the dissension among the patricians, the plebs on his [Duillius's] advice departed from the Aventine and went to the Sacred Mount.[60] Said Duillius also told them that the patricians, until the moment when they would see them abandon the city, would place no concern or care in these matters; that the Sacred Mount would remind them of the constancy of the plebs; and that things could not return to concord until the power of the plebs had first been restored. In other words, they must elect tribunes and issue an appeal to justice.

Comment li dihomme furent debouté et demis de leur magistrat et de leur seigneurie .xxviii. [Ch. 28]

(par. 10) Li ols des cheualiers se est partiz de Aventin et s'en alla par la Voie Numentine que l'en appelloit Figulensi[58] et mist ses tentes en la Montaingne Sainte sanz nulles choses autrement violer, ressemblans l'attemprance de les premiers pers. Et [f. 55rb] touz li plebes[59] les a suivis apréz sanz ce que il y eust nul qui recusast qui[60] fust de aage de aler aprez les autres, si vont aprez fames et enfanz crianz et complaingnanz miserablement et disoient ces paroles: "A cuy nous porrons nous laissier en celle cité, ou liberté ne chasteté ne pueent este sauvéz?" Et lors, comme solitude non acoustumee eust a Romme fait toutes choses gastes et que ou marchié n'aparut homme fors aucun poy des vieillars et encore, quant li per estoient appellé en senat, le dit marchié apparissoit desert, pluseurs en y avoit qui ja crioient plus que Valeres et Oraces et disoient ces mos: "Et que attendrez vous plus, o vous per conscript? Se li dy homme[61] ne veulent faire fin a leur emprise pertinace et obstinee, voulez vous pour ce souffrir toutes choses decheoir[62] et perillier? Et aussi vous, dy homme, quele est ceste seignourie que vous si obstineement embraciez et tenez? Donques, ne voulez vous rendre voz drois aus maisons et aus paroys tant seulement et n'avez vous vergoingne que le nombre de voz licteurs est plus grans ou marchié que n'est li nombres des togues ne des autres? Et se li anemi venoient orendroit, que porriez vous faire? Et se li plebes,[63] veans que par leur cecessions nous ne nous mouvons point, vient seur nous tous armez, volez vous finer vostre empire o le deffinement de ceste cité? Et cuidiez vous tant faire, ce disoient il, que li plebez[64] n'ait jamais ces tribuns? Certes, disoient il, il les doivent avoir ou non. Il avendroit[65] avant que nous serions[66] sanz magistras patriciens que eulx sanz plebeyens. Ceste nouvelle puissance tribunicial, ce disoient il, extorsirent jadiz li plebeyen a noz pers. Et a present eulz, une fois allechié par la douceur, d'icelle ne se deslesseront[67] point, meesmement que il voient[68] que nous ne mettons[69]

---

58   Configulensi *O*; corr. *G*

59   pueples *O*; corr. **GJ**

60   sescusast quil *O*; corr. **GJ**

61   homme *om. O*; corr. *G*. The copyist has placed a slash (/) after "dy" and has indicated in the righthand margin "/.hôme."

62   decheon *O*; corr. *G*

63   pueples *O*; corr. **GJ**

64   pueples *O*; corr. **GJ**

65   avendra *O*; corr. **GJ**

66   serons *O*; corr. **GJ**

67   doulouseront *O*; corr. **GJ**

68   veoient *O*; corr. **GJ**

69   metions *O*; corr. **GJ**

How the decemvirs were chased out of and discharged from their magistracy and from their sovereignty (Ch. 28)

(par. 10) The army of knights departed from the Aventine and went by way of the Via Nomentana, which was called Ficulensis,[61] and placed its encampment at the Sacred Mount without otherwise damaging anything, resembling in this the self-restraint of the ancestral fathers [*les premiers pers*].[62] All the plebs followed behind them without there being any, provided they were of age, who refused to go after the others; and wives with crying children went after them, complaining miserably, and spoke these words: "To whom may we entrust ourselves in this city, in which neither liberty nor chastity can be saved?" Then, as an unaccustomed solitude caused all things to be abandoned in Rome, and as no man appeared in the marketplace other than a certain few of the old men, and moreover as the said marketplace appeared deserted when the senators [*li per*] were called into the Senate, there were then many more than Valerius and Horatius who cried out and spoke these words: "How much longer are you going to wait, oh you conscript fathers [*per conscript*]?[63] If the decemvirs do not wish to bring an end to their relentless and obstinate enterprise, do you wish on this account to allow all things to fall to pieces and perish? And you also, decemvirs, what is this sovereignty that you so obstinately embrace and hold on to? What then, do you not wish to render your judgments to houses and walls alone,[64] and are you not ashamed that the number of your lictors is greater in the marketplace than the number of civilians [*togues*] or others? If the enemies came right now, what would they be able to do about it? And if the plebs, seeing that we are in no way moved by their secession, come upon us fully armed, do you wish to end your rule with the downfall of this city? And do you think you can do enough," they said, "that the plebs may never have these tribunes? Certainly," they said, "they must either have them or not. It would sooner happen that we would be without patrician magistrates than that they would be without plebeian ones. This new tribunician power," they said, "the plebeians extorted it in the past from our forefathers [*pers*]. Having been drawn in by its charm in the past, they will in no way give it up in the present, especially since they can see

nulle atrempance en nostre empire, affin que il aient[70] mainz mestier de l'aide tribunicial." **(par. 11)** Comme ces paroles fussent de toutes pars recitees et dites, li dy homme, vaincu par l'assentement de touz, affermerent que, puis que ainsi leur sembloit, il voloient estre a la volenté et ou pouoir des pers; mais que d'une chose les prioient il et admonnestoient que l'en les gardast d'injure et d'envie et que en leur sanc il ne acoustumassent pas le plebe aus tourmens des pers. Et lors Oraces et Valeres ont esté envoié au pueple revoquer et aus choses acorder par celles condicions qui leur sembleroient convenables, et aussi a l'en commandé que li dy homme fussent gardé de toute violence et de l'esbrivement de la multitude. Les quelz dessus diz Valeres et Oraces y sont allé et a tres grant joie ont esté receu es tentes du plebe, si leur ont esté graces rendues, [f. 55vc] comme a delivreurs du plebe, tant au commencement comme a la fin de la besoingne. Si parla Icilius pour la multitude, et li legat demandoient quelle chose ce estoit que li plebes demandoit et leur fu respondu par le conseil qui avoit esté fait tout avant que l'en se partist du Mont Aventin, quer ce estoit leur entente de meitre plus leur esperance en egauté que en armes, et en raison que en force. Et pour ce il repetoient et demandoient la puissance tribunicial et le privilege de provocacion, les quelles choses avoient esté avant la creation des dix hommes confort et aide du plebe[71] rommain, et affin que il apparust[72] que la secession du pleibe n'estoit pas faite par fraude pour repeter la dite liberté, il demandoient que li dy homme fussent pugny et livré a torment, si que moult en y avoit qui demandoient que il fussent ars touz vis et que ce estoit chose tres raisonnable. **(par. 12)** Li legat dessus dit leur ont ainsi respondu: "Seigneur, distrent il, quant aus choses que vous demandez, par conseil nous vous disons que vous demandez choses si egalz que l'en les vous deust ottroier de bon gré, comme ce soient les deffenses de vostre liberté. Mais quant a ce que vous demandez licence a impugner les autres, doit l'en plus pardonner a vostre ire que li donner liberté de nuyre, meesmement que vous pour hayne de cruauté cheyez et trebuchiez en cruauté. Et par poy, avant que vous soiez delivre et franc, vous volez desja seignourir a voz adversaires. Vostre cité, distrent il, ne puet avoir repos de tourmens et de painnes l'un a l'autre inferer, ou des pers en plebe[73] ou du plebe[74] es pers, si que il semble[75] que vous eussiez miex besoing d'escu que de glayve et si est assez simples et humbles qui illueques puet vivre en pais et sanz faire et sanz[76] soustrire injure. Et certes, disoient il, se vous aucune fois volez faire nulle chose de rigueur et vous moustrer telx que l'en vous doie craindre, si devez atendre que vous aiés

---

70   eussent *O*; corr. **GJ**
71   pueple *O*; corr. *GJ*
72   apparut *O*; corr. *GJ*
73   pueple *O*; corr. *GJ*
74   pueple *O*; corr. *GJ*
75   sembloit *O*; corr. *G*
76   sanz *om. O*; corr. **GJ**

that we have imposed no moderation on our power, in order that they might have less need of tribunician help." **(par. 11)** As these speeches were repeated and spoken all over the place, the decemvirs, defeated by the assent of all, affirmed that, as seemed good to them [the senators], they wished to be at the will and under the power of the senators [*pers*]; yet they pleaded with them and urged for one certain thing, that they be protected from injury and malice and that through their blood they might not accustom the plebs to the torturing of patricians. Then Horatius and Valerius were sent to recall the people[65] and to strike agreements under such conditions as seemed suitable to them; also, it was ordered that the decemvirs be protected from any violence and from the assault of the crowd. The aforementioned Valerius and Horatius went to the encampment of the plebs, were received there with very great joy, and were offered thanks, as if to the saviors of the plebs, as much at the beginning of the affair as at the end. Icilius spoke for the crowd, and when the legates asked what it was the plebs demanded, they received in reply the advice that had been given even before they left the Aventine Hill, that their intention was to place their hope in equity more than in arms, and in reason more than in force.[66] For this reason, they claimed and demanded tribunician power and the right of appeal, which had been a comfort and aid to the Roman plebs before the election of the decemvirs; and so that it would not appear that the secession of the plebs had been done through fraud to claim said liberty, they demanded that the decemvirs be punished and rendered to torture; indeed, there were many who demanded that they be burned alive, saying that this was a very reasonable thing.[67] **(par. 12)** The aforementioned legates responded to them thus: "Lords," they said, "as for the things you demand, we tell you this upon reflection, that you ask for such equitable things that one ought to grant them to you willingly, as they are the means of defending your liberty. But as for your demanding license to attack others, one ought to forgive you your ire more than grant you the liberty to cause harm, especially when out of hatred of cruelty you fall and slip into cruelty.[68] Almost before being liberated and set free, you already wish to rule over your adversaries. Your city," they said, "will not have respite from the torments and pains the one inflicts on the other, be it patricians on plebs or plebs on patricians, in such a way that it seems that you would have greater need of a shield than of a sword; and indeed, whoever is able to live there in peace, without causing or undergoing injury, is truly decent and humble.[69] Certainly," they said, "if at some point you wish to do nothing out of excessive harshness and wish to show yourselves in such a way that people must fear you, then you should wait until you have recovered

recouvré voz[77] magistraux et voz loys et que li jugement de noz[78] et de nos[79] fortunes soient en vostre main, et lors vous ordonnerez de chascun selonc ce que droiz sera. Mais quant ad present, distrent il, vous doit il bien sousfire repeter liberté."

Comment nouveaux tribuns plebeyens furent creez .xxix. [Ch. 29]

(par. 13) Ces choses oyes, li plebes a ottroié aus legas que il feissent ce que il vorroient, si leur ont dit li legat que il reporteroient au senat leur response et que tantost il tourneroient vers eulz. Et quant il s'en furent allé devers les pers et reporté la volenté du plebe tuit li dy homme, excepté Appius, veans que de leurs painnes ne faisoit on nulles mensions, dirrent que il ne refuseroient nulle chose qui par le senat leur fust commandee. Mais li dis Appius, qui estoit homs de fier et de aspre engin considerans par la haine es autres [f. 55vd] la hayne d'eulz en soy, a dit ces paroles: "Fortune, dist il, seurvient a celui qui bien la sent venir. Je voy bien, dist il, que jusques atant que nous baillons noz armes a noz anemis il delaient de eulz combatre a nous, mais nyentmainz pour ce ne lerai je mie de moy demettre de cest decemvirat." (par. 14) Lors fu fait un conseil de senat et une ordenance que avant toute oeuvre li dy homme renonçassent a leur osfice et que Quincius li souverainz evesques creast tribuns de plebe et en oultre que la dite secession des chevaliers de tribuns et de plebe et leur departie du pouoir des dix homes ne peust jamais a nullui estre imputee avoir esté faite par fraude. Et ces ordenances faites et laissié le senat,[80] li dy homme s'en issirent en parlement publique et renoncierent publiquement a leur magistrat. Si furent ces choses denonciees a tres grant joie au plebe[81] et suyrent les legas tuit cil qui estoient demouré en la cité et a ceste multitude issant[82] de la ville vint a l'encontre joieusement l'autre multitude qui estoit es tentes et se esjoissoient ensemble de concorde et de liberté qui estoient restituez a la cité. (par. 15) Li legat se pristrent a aparler[83] le plebe et distrent ces paroles: "Seigneur, distrent il, que bon eur et bien fortune soit a vous et a l'estat commun. Tournez vous ent en vostre pays chascun en son hostel a voz fames et a voz enfans et gardez que vostre retour soit o telle attemprance comme a esté vostre demeure en laquelle en tant de choses neccessaires a si grant multitude le champ de nuluy n'a esté violé. Alez vous

---

[77]   que l'en vous …recouvré voz *om. O*; corr. *G*
[78]   *O* has written *nous* and crossed it out with dots, putting *noz* in the margin; noz *J*; vous *G*
[79]   voz *OG*; corr. *J*
[80]   et laissié le senat *placed after* departie *O*; corr. *G*
[81]   pueple *O*; corr. *GJ*
[82]   issent *O*; corr. *G*
[83]   a a parle *O*; corr. *G*

your magistrates and your laws and until jurisdiction over us and over our fortunes is in your hands; then you will ordain what will be right for each man. But as for the present," they said, "it must be enough for you to claim liberty."

How new plebeian tribunes were elected (Ch. 29)

(par. 13) Having heard these things, the plebs granted that the legates might do what they wished; and the legates told them they would report their response to the Senate and would return to them soon thereafter. When they had gone before the senators [*li pers*] and reported the will of the plebs, all the decemvirs, except Appius, seeing that no mention was made of their punishments, said that they would refuse nothing that the Senate might command of them. But Appius, who was a man of cruel and harsh disposition, assessing the hatred of others by his own hatred of them, spoke these words: "Fortune," he said, "comes to the aid of he who senses well that she is coming. I fully understand," he said, "that our enemies are waiting to attack us until we have given up our arms;[70] but nonetheless, I will not because of this fail to renounce my position in this decemvirate."[71] (par. 14) Then a Senatorial decree was made and an order issued that the decemvirs would renounce their office without delay and that Quintus [Furius], the ruling bishop,[72] would hold an election for tribunes of the plebs and in addition that the said secession of the tribunes of the knights and of the plebs and their removal of the decemvirs from power ought never to be imputed to anyone as having been done through fraud.[73] These orders having been issued and the Senate disbanded, the decemvirs went out into a public assembly and publicly renounced their magistracy. These things were announced with very great joy to the plebs, and all those who had remained in the city followed the legates. This crowd issuing forth from the city met with joy the other crowd, which was at the encampment and was rejoicing together on account of the concord and liberty that had been restored to the city. (par. 15) The legates began to address the plebs and spoke these words: "Lords," they said, "may you and the common estate have good luck and good fortune. Return to your land, with each man in his home, and return to your wives and your children; and take care that you make your return with the same self-restraint you have dwelled in here as so many necessary matters were settled for so great a crowd without anyone's estate having been plundered. Go straight to the Aventine Hill from which

ent droit ou Mont Aventin dont vous partistes et illueques ou vous empreistes les commencemens de vostre liberté vous creerez[84] voz tribuns et illueques sera tous prests li souverainz evesques qui vous avra[85] comices." **(par. 16)** Grans assentemens et grans alegrece fu illueques veue et touz aprouverent[86] l'ordenance des legas et tournerent leurs banieres et s'en allerent en la cité et se combatoient de joie a ceulz que il encontroient et passans coiement par mi la cité vindrent jusques en Aventin, ou quel lieu, le grant evesque tenant ses comices, il ont tantost créé tribuns de pueple qui furent ceulz: ce furent Aulus Virginius, L. Ycilius, P. Munitorius, oncles du dit Virginius qui avoient esté aucteurs de la sedicion, et aprez ceulz G. Sictinius, qui estoit du lignage de celui premier tribun qui jaidis avoit esté créez en la Sainte Montaingne, et, aveuques eulz, M. Diulium qui, avant les dix homes créez, avoit eu notable tribunat ne en debas decemviraux n'avoit onques failli au plebe. Et aveuques ceulz ci, furent esleu, plus par esperance de bien faire ou temps a venir que pour merites du temps passé, M. Ticinius, M. Pomponius, E. Appronius, [f. 56ra] Appius Villius, G. Oppius. Et tantost commencié l'osfice du dit tribunat, li dis Icilius requist le plebe et li plebes le assenti et determina que la secession faite du pouoir des dix homes ne peust jamais a nulluy estre imputee a crime ne a fraude, ainçois que elle fust de touz poinz pardonnee . Et tantost apréz cecy Marcus Duillius fist requeste que l'en creast consulz aveuques provocation et furent toutes choses faites par le per Flamin, qui ores est appellez Circum Flamius, c'estoit le grant evesque et en conseil du pleibe.

Ci parle de la discorde qui fu entre les peres et les tribuns plebeyens .xxx. [Ch. 30]

(.C. xv [Ch. 15]) (par. 1)[87] Aprez les dix homes demis et despoulliez de leur osfice, ce fu l'an trois cenz et cinq aprez Romme fondee, par l'interroy, c'est a dire par celui qui, aprez la resignation des dix hommes, avoit esté establis gouverneur des besongnes[88] publiques jusques a la creation des consuls, furent créez consulz L. Valerius et M. Horacius, qui tantost commencierent a excercer leur office, des quelz li consulaz fu populaires et favourables au plebe[89] sanz nulle injure des pers, mais non pas sanz l'offence d'eulx. Car

84   croirez *O*; corr. *G*
85   avra *O*; tenra *G*.
86   tout approuveroit *O*; corr. *G*
87   See above note 32.
88   negoces *G*
89   pueple *O*; corr. *GJ*

you departed and where you undertook the beginnings of your liberty. You will elect your tribunes, and there at the ready will be the ruling bishop who will hold the comitium for you." **(par. 16)** Great approbation and great joy were seen there; all approved the legates' order and turned their banners and left the city and competed with those they encountered in expressing joy. Moving peacefully through the city, they came to the Aventine, at which place the great bishop was holding his comitium. They soon elected tribunes of the people,[74] who were these men: Aulus [Lucius] Verginius, L[ucius] Icilius, and P[ublius] Munitorius [Numitorius], who were uncles of said Verginius and authors of the sedition;[75] and after these men, G[aius] Sictinius [Sicinius], who was of the lineage of the first tribune, who long ago was elected on the Sacred Mount; and with these men, M[arcus] Diulium [Duillius], who had been a notable tribune before the decemvirs were elected and had never failed the plebs in struggles with the decemvirs. With these men were elected, more out of hope of good deeds in times to come than on account of merits from times passed, M[arcus] Ticinius [Titinius], M[arcus] Pomponius, E. [Gaius] Appronius [Apronius], Appius Villius, and G[aius] Oppius. As soon as they had taken the office of the said tribunate, said Icilius proposed to the plebs, and the plebs assented to it and decreed, that the withdrawal of power from the decemvirs ought never to be imputed to anyone as a crime or as fraud, such that it might be pardoned in every respect. Soon thereafter, this Marcus Duillius made a motion that consuls should be elected subject to appeal, and all these things were carried out by the patrician Flamin[ius],[76] for whom the Circus Flami[ni]us[77] is now named; he was a great bishop and was on the council of the plebs.

Here the text speaks of the discord between the patricians and the plebeian tribunes (Ch. 30)[78]

(Ch. 15) (par. 1) After the decemvirs were deposed and removed from their office, in the year three hundred and five after Rome was founded,[79] L[ucius] Valerius and M[arcus] Horatius were elected consuls by an interrex, that is by he who, after the resignation of the decemvirs, had been installed as governor of public affairs until the election of the consuls; they immediately began to exercise their office, and thanks to them, the consular regime was popular and favorable to the plebs, without causing any harm to the patricians, though it did not fail to receive attacks from the latter. For whatever they viewed

tout ce que il veoient estre fait en faveur de la liberté du plebe,[90] il reputoient estre fait ou prejudice d'eulz. Dont comme avant toutes choses il fu entre eulz controversie, savoir mon, se les pers estoient tenuz d'obeir aus establissemens du plebe,[91] les quelz l'en appelloit plebiscitez, li diz consulz,[92] par comicez centuriez, establirent une loy, que ce que li tribuns du plebe commandast, touz li pueples tenist la quelle loy; fu des lors en avant uns tres aspres javelos aus tribuns, contre les pers en toutes leurs demandes. Et aussi l'autre loy de provocation, la quelle estoit une seule aide et une seule deffense de liberté, et la quelle avoit esté destruite par le pouoir des dix hommes, ne restituerent pas seulement le dit consul, ainçois le fermerent et garnirent pour le temps a venir en establissant une nouvelle loy, que des lors en avant nulz magistrax ne fust créez sanz provocation et que quiconques le creast il leiast a chascun occirre celui createur, sanz ce que l'en en fust tenuz de crime capital. (par. 2) Et comme li consul eussent sousfisaument fermé le plebe,[93] tant par l'ayde tribunicial comme par la dite loy de provocacion, si renouvelerent en oultre le privilege des tribuns par aucunes cerimonies, li quelz par lonc intervalle avoit esté aussi comme mis en oubli. C'est a dire que il fussent reputé sacrosaint, si comme li premier tribun avoient esté. Et que durant leur office nulz ne les osast envaïr ne touchier. Et establirent par loy et par statu que quiconques violeroit nulz tribuns de plebe, ediles, jugez et dix hommes, se autres fois avenoit que il fussent créé, sa teste fust sacrifiee a Jupiter, c'est a dire [f. 56rb] que il fust decapitez et en oultre que sa fame, ses enfans, et sa famille feussent vendus et la peccune dediee ou temple de Seres. Et interpreterent aucun que soubs ceste loy oracienne li consul estoient contenu, pour ce que il estoient juge, et aussi voulrent il dire des preteurs, pour ce que il estoient créé a guise des consulz . Et si y ot aucuns qui voulrent dire que ceste loy ne devoit pas ainsi estre entendue pour ce que li edille n'apparoient pas estre sacrosaint, pour ce que li autre magistrat les prenoient et metoient em prison bien souvent. Et aussi li dit consul firent une autre loy, car les establissemens que l'en appelloit consulteniens du senat, les quelz li consul avoient par leur volunté acoustumé a taire ou a destruire afin que des ores il ne peussent perillier, fussent portez ou temple de Ceres et baillié aus edilles et mis en seure garde. (par. 3) Aprez cecy, .M. Duillius, tribuns du plebe, requist le plebe, et li plebes l'establist, que qui laisseroit le plebe sanz tribuns et que qui créeroit nul magistrat sanz provocation fussent pugny de dos et de teste, c'est a dire que il fussent premierement batu de verges et puis descapité. Et ainsi se passerent toutes ces choses contre la volenté des patriciens, ja soit ce que il n'y eussent resisté en rienz pour ce que l'en ne aissailloit encore nulz d'eulz singulierement.

---

[90]   pueple *O*; corr. *GJ*
[91]   pueple *O*; corr. *GJ*
[92]   le dit consul *O*; corr. *G*
[93]   pueple *O*; corr. *GJ*

as being done in favor of the liberty of the plebs, they considered to have been done against their interests. As a result of this, since there was above all discord among them, namely, regarding whether the patricians were bound to obey the rulings of the plebs, which were called plebiscites,[80] the said consuls enacted, through the centuriated assembly,[81] a law stipulating that that which the tribune of the plebs should command, all the people would uphold as legally binding; this law was from then on a very sharp weapon for the tribunes, in response to all the legal petitions of the patricians.[82] Also, the said consuls not only restored the other law, that of the right to appeal, which was a unique aid to and defense of liberty, and which had been destroyed by the power of the decemvirs, but they also fortified and defended it for times to come by establishing a new law stipulating that from then on, no one should declare the election of any magistrate without the right of appeal and that it be permitted for an individual to kill the person who might declare such an election without that individual being held for a capital crime. **(par. 2)** As the consuls had sufficiently strengthened the plebs, as much through tribunician help as through the said law of appeal, in addition they renewed the privilege of the tribunes by certain ceremonies, which for a long period of time had effectively been forgotten. This [privilege] means that they were held to be sacrosanct, as the first tribune had been, and that during their tenure none should dare attack or touch them. They established by law and by statute that whosoever should assault any tribunes of the plebs, aediles,[83] judges, and decemvirs,[84] if it happened that they had already been named [to those posts], his head would be sacrificed to Jupiter, meaning that he would be decapitated and moreover that his wife, his children, and his family would be sold and the money dedicated to the temple of Ceres.[85] Certain men expounded that the consuls were included under this Horatian law, as they were judges; and those men wished to say the same of the praetors also, as they were elected in the same manner as the consuls.[86] There were other men who wished to say that this law ought not to be understood in this way, as the aediles did not appear to be sacrosanct, given that the other magistrates rather often seized them and put them in prison. Also, the said consuls created another law, regarding the orders that were called *senatus consulta*,[87] which the consuls had been accustomed to willfully silence or destroy; henceforth, so that they might not be endangered, they were to be carried to the Temple of Ceres, delivered to the aediles, and placed under secure guard. **(par. 3)** After this, M[arcus] Duillius, tribune of the plebs, proposed to the plebs, and the plebs so ordered, that whoever would leave the plebs without tribunes and whoever would declare the election of any magistrate without the right of appeal should receive the penalty on the back and the head; in other words, they should first be beaten with rods and then decapitated. All these matters were approved against the will of the patricians, yet they had not in any way attempted to block these measures since none of them had yet been attacked individually.

Comment Appius fu cité a respondre a Virginius et comment il vint en jugement
.xxxi. [Ch. 31]

Si avint, aprez ce que la puissance tribunicial fu fondee et aussi la liberté du
plebe,[94] li tribun considererent que il estoit heure de envayr les coulpables.
Et pour ce, tout au premier, il ordenerent Virginium comme accuseur contre
Appius Claudius dessus dit. Et comme Virginius eust dit et donnee journee
criminelment au dit Appius, et li dis Appius, chainz a l'entour de grant
compaingnie de jouvenciaux patriciens, fust descenduz ou marchié pendant
a sa journee, tantost que l'en vit luy et ses [95] satellites, fu renterinee et ravisee
la memoire de son honni pouoir. Si dit Virginius ces paroles: "Seigneurs, dist
il, oroison ou pleidoierie furent trouvees pour choses doubteuses et non pour
choses cleres. Et pour ce, dist it, que je ne gaste pas mon temps sanz raison
en accusant cestuy de la cuy cruauté il vous a convenu vous delivrer par force
d'armes, je ne li entenz pas ad present opposer pluseurs et divers crimes affin
que il ne multiplie son obstination en plaidoiant et en soy desfendant, la quelle
chose je n'entens pas a sousfrir. Et pour ce, dist il, O tu Appi, de tous les
maulx que tu par l'espasse de deux ans as osé faire et cruelment commeitre
en cumulant l'un seur l'autre, je te fais grace fors d'un [f. 56vc] tout seul, du
quel je entens a demander et a prendre venjance. Et pour ce, afin que tu ne dies
en toy escusant que tu ne donnaz mie les vindices contre les loys, c'est a dire
les sentences ainsi appellees pour ma fille amener de liberté en servitude, je
commande avant toutes choses que tu soies pris et mis en lyens."

Vindices estoient les verges des licteurs que l'en mettoit sur la teste de celuy
franc que l'en demandoit estre serf, ou de celi serf que l'en demandoit
estre franc. Aussi, les sentences seur ce donnees furent dites "vindices."[96]

(par. 4) Appius, regardanz que en l'ayde tribunicial ne ou jugement du
pueple[97] ne avoit il point d'esperance, appella aus autres tribuns, mais
comme nulz d'eulx ne li donnast secours, li sergens voiers a mis main a luy
et si a dit Appius derrechief, "je appelle." Si fist lors silence celle vois de
franchise, ja soit ce que elle fust issue de celle bouche dont les vindices contre
franchise avoient esté dites et jugiees, n'avoit pas gramm_ent. Endementres
que chascuns fremissoit et murmuroit contre le dit Appius, en merciant les
dieux de ce que il avoient memoire de eulx et de ce que il ne mesprisoient

94   pueple *O*; corr. *GJ*
95   s. lecaious ou s. *O*; corr. *G*
96   Placed in left hand margin of first column, in gothic script, same as that of the main
text
97   plebe *GJ*

How Appius was summoned to undergo Verginius's interrogation, and how he appeared at his trial (Ch. 31)

It then came about that, after the tribunician authority was established along with the liberty of the plebs, the tribunes considered it time to prosecute the guilty. To do so, first, they ordered Verginius to appear as plaintiff against the aforementioned Appius Claudius. When Verginius had fixed a court date and announced it to said Appius, and when said Appius, surrounded on all sides by a large company of young patrician men, had arrived at the forum on the appointed day, the memory of his contemptible power was restored and brought back to mind as soon as people saw him and his henchmen. Verginius spoke these words: "Lords," he said, "oratory and pleas were invented for doubtful matters rather than clear ones. So that I may not waste my time for no reason by accusing this man from whose cruelty it suited you to free yourself by force of arms, I do not intend at present to accuse him of many, diverse crimes lest he increase his obstinacy by pleading his case and defending himself, something I have no intention of tolerating. For this reason," he said, "oh you, Appius, I forgive you for all the wrongs you dared to perpetrate over the space of two years and that you cruelly committed, accumulating them one upon the other; for all the wrongs except one and one alone, for which I intend to seek and impose retribution. For this reason, so that you may not justify yourself by saying that you in no way applied the vindices unlawfully, that is, the sentence issued to lead my daughter from liberty into servitude, I order before all else that you be seized and placed in fetters."

Marginal Note: Vindices were the lictors' rods, which they placed on the head of a free man who was claimed as a slave, or of a slave who was claimed as free. Also, the verdicts given on such matters were called "the vindices."[88]

(par. 4) Appius, seeing that he had not the least hope of tribunician aid nor of a judgment from the people, appealed to the other tribunes; but as none of them gave him help, the *viator*[89] placed his hand upon him and Appius thereupon said, "I appeal." This expression of freedom then caused a silence to fall, even though it had issued from that mouth that had spoken and pronounced the vindices against freedom not long before. In the meantime, each man shuddered and muttered against said Appius, thanking the gods for having remembered them and for not having disdained the governance of human

pas le gouvernement des choses humainnes et de ce que il veoient avenir a orgueil et a crualté painnes non pas legieres, combien que elles tarjassent. "Or veons nous, disoient il, que Appius provoque et appelle, qui avoit a touz osté et soustrait le remede de provocation, et que celuy supplioit le secours et l'ayde du pueple qui touz les drois du pueple avoit anoienté et que celuy, ravis en liens, si veult jouir du[98] droit de liberté et de franchise qui la personne franche avoit l'autrier sousmis a servitute." **(par. 5)** Toutes voies entre ces choses estoit oye la vois de Appius qui remembroit les merites de ses parens en la chose publique, tant en tans de pais comme en tamps de guerre, et aussi recordoit il son maleureux estude vers le pueple romain, qui pour leurs loys assembler avoit laissié le consulat contre la volenté des pers – "les quelles loys, ce disoit il, demourans en leur estat, je, li faiseurs d'icelles, suy menez en lyens." Et requeroit li diz Appius que il li appartenoit[99] experir et asseoir ses biens et ses maulz en la presence de touz, et que[100] comme l'en li ait donné faculté et pouoir de respondre a certain jour, il requeroit que par le commun droit de la cité, entre deux, il feust gouvernez comme cytoiens de Romme. Et disoit plus que il n'avoit pas tant doubté le jugement du plebe[101] que il n'ait tousjours[102] bonne esperance en la misericorde de ses cytoiens. Et pour ce voloit conclurre que avant le jour l'en ne le devoit pas lier ne encheinier,[103] la quele chose, se l'en li voloit faire, il appelloit derrechief aus tribuns et au plebe,[104] et les admonnestoit que il ne voulsissent pas ressembler ceulz que il[105] heoient. "Et se li tribun ne me veulent oïr en m'appellacion, il me semble que il se confessent estre coulpabes[106] de celle chose [f. 56vd] meismes dont il blasmoient les dix hommes, c'est a dire de tolir le remede de provocacion," et pour ce disoit il que il provoquoit au pueple romain et requeroit l'ayde des loys tribuniciaux et consulaires qui, seur ce, avoient esté faites celle meismes annee. "O, disoit il, et se il ne m'apartient de[107] provoquer pendant le jour de ma cause avant que soie condempnez, comme l'apartendra[108] il faire a un povre homme plebeyen? Et comment[109] trouvera secours ne aide en loys se Appius Claudius ne le puet trouver? Orendroit, disoit il, porrez vous prouver

    [98] "de" in text is corrected (with two dots under the letters) to "du" written in the left margin
    [99] il li loist *G*
    [100] que *om. O*; corr. *GJ*
    [101] pueple *O*; corr. *GJ*
    [102] t. eu *O*; corr. *G*
    [103] enchaienner *G*
    [104] pueple *O*; corr. *GJ*
    [105] qui le *O*; corr. *G*
    [106] semblables et coupables *G*
    [107] me loist *G*
    [108] le loyst *G*
    [109] comme *O*; corr. *G*

affairs, for they saw that pride and cruelty receive penalties that were in no way lenient, even if they were delayed. "Let us now recognize," they said, "that Appius challenges and appeals, he who had removed and withheld the remedy of appeal from everyone; that this man who had nullified all the rights of the people was imploring the assistance and aid of the people; and that he who wishes to enjoy the right of liberty and of freedom, even as he is carried off in chains, just the other day subjected the person of a free citizen to slavery." **(par. 5)** Nonetheless, among these things was heard the voice of Appius, who recalled the contributions of his ancestors in public affairs [*en la chose publique*], as much in times of peace as in times of war; and he also recalled his unfortunate zeal toward the Roman people,[90] he who had assembled their laws, abandoning the consulship against the will of the patricians – "which laws," he said, "remain in place even as I, their maker, am carried off in fetters." Said Appius pleaded that it would be fitting for him to put to the test and establish his good and bad deeds in the presence of all; and that seeing as they had given him the ability and possibility to testify on a specific day, he pleaded that by the common right of the city, he ought to be governed in the meantime as a citizen of Rome. He further said that he had not feared the judgment of the plebs so much that he did not continue to have good hope in the mercy of his fellow citizens. For this reason, he wished to conclude that before the appointed day they ought not to fetter or chain him; but if they wished to do this thing to him, he would instantly appeal once again to the tribunes and the plebs;[91] and he furthermore admonished them that they should not wish to resemble those whom they hated. "If the tribunes do not wish to hear me in my appeal, it seems to me that they confess themselves to be guilty of this very thing they blamed on the decemvirs, that is taking away the remedy of appeal"; and for this reason, he said that he appealed to the Roman people and implored the support of the tribunician and consular laws that, regarding this matter, had been established that very year. "Oh," he said, "and if it is not appropriate for me to appeal on the day of my case, before I can be condemned, how will it be appropriate for a poor plebeian man to do so? How will he find either hope or aid in the laws if Appius Claudius cannot find it? Now," he said, "are you able to prove in my case whether liberty or

en moy se par voz loys nouvelles franchise ou seignourie ont esté confermees et se appellation ou provocation, qui ont esté ottroiees a franchise contre l'injure des magistraz, ont esté tant seulement bolanciees par vainnes paroles ou escriptes en vainnes lettres."

La response de Virginius contre Appius, le quel Appius fu mis en prison .xxxii. [Ch. 32]

(**par. 6**) Contre ces choses dites, respont Virginius et dit ainsi: "Seigneurs, dist il, je say bien que cestuy Appius Claudius que vous avez oy parler, si comme il semble, est non savans et inexpers de toute civile et humainne aliance. Et pour Dieu,[110] disoit il, regardez son siege judicial comme ce estoit un chastel et une desfense de toutes malvaistiez, en quel lieu cestuy dy homme, qui cuidoit estre durans et pardurables, comme convoiteux du dos et du sanc de ses cytoiens et donnans menaces a touz bons de verges et coingnies, mespriseurs des dieux et des hommes, avironnez de bouchers non pas de licteurs, tresporte son courage de rappines et de occision a ribauderie: ravit la vierge franche d'entre les bras son pere en la presence du pueple romain. Et aussi comme se elle fust serve prise en bataille, il la donna et adjuga a son sergent et a son chambellein, et ou quel lieu par son cruel decret et par ses vindices iniques et neffandes, il arma la destre du pere en sa propre fille et ou quel lieu l'espous et l'aieil de la vierge, qui emportoient son corps qui estoit aussi comme sanz ame, il commanda mener em prison, plus esmeus pour cause de sa luxure empeschiee que pour cause de l'occision[111] de la demoiselle. Et en celuy lieu fist chartre edifier que il avoit acoustumé apeller l'ostel du plebe[112] romain. Et pour ce se plusieurs fois derrechief et derrechief il provoque tousjours, je li diray que je suy pres de luy oyr se ainsi n'est[113] que il n'ait donné vindices de liberté en servitute, et ainsi que pour nyent demande soy joïr[114] de provocation, qui est previlege de liberté comme il l'ait[115] si injustement impugnee. Et pour ce que ceste chose il ne porroit nyer, je weil et commande, dist Virginius, que il soit menez en lyens comme convaincus de ceste chose." Si fu tantost li dis Appius pris et menez em prison sanz ce que nulz se meist au devant ou deist que ce fust malfait a grant mouvement de [f. 57ra] courages, pour ce que a chascun sembloit que la liberté du plebe[116] estoit ja tresgrande, puis que il pouoit si[117] grant homme pugnir et enchartrer, si li alonga[118] li tribuns le jour de son jugement.

[110] Dieu *om. O;* corr. *G*
[111] l'occasion *O;* corr. *G*
[112] pueple *O;* corr. *JG*
[113] est *GJ*
[114] ouir *O;* corr. *GJ*
[115] loyt *O;* corr. *G*
[116] pueple *O;* corr. *GJ*
[117] si *om. O;* corr. *GJ*
[118] alongna *G*

domination have been confirmed in your new laws and whether petition and appeal, which were granted for the sake of freedom against the injustice of the magistrates, have quite simply been cast aside through empty words or written down in empty letters."

The testimony of Verginius against Appius, who was thrown in prison (Ch. 32)

(par. 6) Countering these things that were said, Verginius responds and speaks thus: "Lords," he said, "I know well that this Appius Claudius whom you have heard speak is, as it seems, ignorant of and inexperienced in all civil and human alliance. And for God's sake," he said, "consider his judicial seat and how it has been a fortress and stronghold for all sorts of misdeeds, a place in which this decemvir, who thought himself to be enduring and perpetual, as if covetous of the backs and blood of his fellow citizens and issuing threats against all good people with rods and axes, scornful of gods and men, surrounded by butchers rather than lictors, turns his thoughts from plunder and murder to debauchery: he abducted the free virgin from her father's arms in the presence of the Roman people. Just as if she were a slave seized in battle, he gave and granted her to his officer and chamberlain. And in this place [the judicial seat], by his cruel decree and by his iniquitous and nefarious use of the vindices, he armed the right hand of the father against his own daughter; and in this place, he commanded that the groom and the grandfather of the virgin, they who carried off her body, which appeared to be lifeless, be themselves carried off to prison, moved more by his thwarted lust than by the murder of the maiden. And in this place, he ordered a prison erected that he was accustomed to calling the home of the Roman plebs.[92] It is for this reason that, if he endlessly appeals, over and over many times, I will tell him that I am ready to hear him if it is not the case that he pronounced the sentence of the vindices, turning liberty into slavery; but that, according to this, he asks to no avail to benefit from the right of appeal, which is the privilege of liberty that he so unjustly attacked. Given that he could not deny this thing, I wish and command," said Verginius, "that he be led away in fetters as a man convicted of this charge." Thus, said Appius was immediately seized and led away to prison without any man raising objections or saying that it was wrong; there was a great stirring of opinions, inasmuch as it seemed to everyone that the liberty of the plebs was already very great, given that they could punish and imprison so great a man. And so, the tribune deferred the day of his judgment.

(par. 7) Endementres que ces choses se demenoient, li Latin et li Hernicien tramistrent leurs legas a Romme a conjouir et a congratuler de la concorde des pers et du plebe;[119] et pour ce il aporterent un don a Jupiter le tresgrant et tresbon. Ce fu une couronne d'or assez de petit pois, si comme la fortune de eulz le requeroit par celli temps, la quele il osfrirent en capitole. Car a celi temps l'en coustivoit les religions[120] plus pieument que manificement. Et par ces legas fu aussi congneu que li Volsque et li Eque par souverainne force aprestoient bataille, pour la quelle chose l'en commanda aus consulz partir les provinces, si avint a Orace la province sabine, et a Valeres la province des Eques. Et comme li dit consul eussent fait crier le delect pour descripre leur ost a celles guerres, la faveur du plebe[121] fu si grant que non pas li juveneur[122] seulement mais, avec ce, li chevalier ancien et emerit et grant partie d'autres de bonne volenté furent tous pres a baillier leurs noms, si que celluy ost fu moult fort et moult ferme, non pas seulement pour la plenté mais, aveuques ce, par la value des chevaliers viellars[123] et esprovez qui y estoient merlez. Mais tout avant que il ississent de la cité, les loys decemviraux que l'en appelloit les lois des douze tables, furent escriptes en arain et proposees en publique, et ce fu fait selonc aucuns par l'office des ediles.

Comment Quincius Claudius, pere de Appius, requist piteusement le pueple pour la delivrance de son filz Appius, le quel Appius mourut avant le jour de son jugement .xxxiii. [Ch. 33]

(par. 8) G. Claudius, li peres Appius, qui pour la hayne des tors fais des diz homes et qui, seur touz les autres, avoit esté contraires a l'orgueil de son filz, s'en estoit allez a Regille, son ancien pays. Cilz, ja de grant eage, estoit venuz a Rome pour remedier aus perilz de son filz, du quel il avoit fuy les vices et les maux. Si vint li proudons, vestuz de robe de duel, aveuques ses sergens et son simple menage et descendi ou marchié, pensans et requerans chascun que pour Dieu il leur pleust[124] avoir pitié de son filz et que a la gent claudienne il ne voulsissent anoncier celle non juste tache, que il fussent veu digne de chartres et de liens. "Seigneurs, disoit il, certes, il n'est pas bien seant que li conditeurs de voz loys et li faiseurs du droit rommain, qui, ou temps a venir, a a estre comme une honouree ymage par reverence des loys, gise orendroit entre les larrons

---

[119] pueple *OG*; corr. *J*
[120] reliques *O*; corr. *GJ*
[121] pueple *O*; corr. *GJ*
[122] les plus jones *O*; corr. *GJ*
[123] vaillans *O*; corr. *GJ*
[124] p. de *O*; corr. *GJ*

(par. 7) At the same time as these things were being debated, the Latins and the Hernici[93] sent their legates to Rome to celebrate and rejoice over the concord between patricians and plebs; and for this reason, they brought a gift for Jupiter Optimus Maximus. As their fortune required of them at that time, it was a crown of gold of rather light weight, which they offered to the Capitol.[94] For at that time, they practiced their religions with more piety than splendor. Through these legates, it was made known that the Volsci and the Aequi were making extreme efforts to prepare for battle; and for this reason, they ordered the consuls to divide up the provinces; thus, the Sabine province fell to Horatius and the Aequi province to Valerius.[95] When the said consuls had proclaimed a raising of troops in order to take the inventory of their army in these wars, the enthusiasm of the plebs was so great that not only the youth alone but also the old, discharged knights and a large share of others of good will were all ready to give their names, such that this army was very strong and very steadfast, not only on account of great numbers but also on account of the power of the elderly and experienced knights who were joined to it. Yet well before they left the city, the decemviral laws that were called the laws of the Twelve Tables were engraved in bronze and presented in public; and according to some, this was done by the office of the aediles.

How Quincius [Gaius] Claudius, father of Appius,[96] piteously implored the people for the deliverance of his son Appius, who died before the day of his judgment (Ch. 33)

(par. 8) G[aius] Claudius, Appius's father, who out of hatred for the tricks played by the decemvirs and who had been, above all others, opposed to his son's arrogance, had gone away to Regillus, his ancestral land. Already advanced in age, he had come to Rome to find a remedy for the perils of his son, whose vices and misdeeds he had fled. Thus, the worthy man arrived, dressed in the garb of woe and accompanied by his officers and simple followers, and went to the marketplace, heavy of heart and imploring everyone to please have pity on his son for God's sake and to choose not to denounce the Claudian clan for this stain of injustice by which they might be viewed as worthy of prisons and fetters. "Lords," he said, "it is certainly not fitting that the creator of your statutes and the maker of Roman law, one who, in times to come, is to be honored in effigy out of reverence for the laws, should at this

diurnes et nocturnes liez et encheennez. Et, pour amour, seigneurs, revirez[125] un poy voz courages de ire a connoissance et a apensement, et voeilliez avant donner cestui seul a tant de claudyens qui [f. 57rb] pour luy vous supplient que pour hayne de luy seul refuser les prieres de tant de vaillanz genz; et faites ceste grace non pas a luy mais au nom claudeain et au lignage de luy. Et ce, disoit il, vous requier je pour mon filz, non pas que il soit tornez en grace aveques moy, mais pour ce que je le voeil secourre, a mon pouoir, a sa fortune adverse. Et certes, ce disoit il, puis que vous avez recouvré liberté par vertu et par force, il est raison que vous la confermez par la debonnaireté et par la concorde des ordres." **(par. 9)** Assez y avoit de ceulz qui pour les paroles du viellart Claudius estoient esmeus et plus pour pitié de luy que de celui pour cui cause il prioit. Mais Virginius prioit le plebe[126] d'autre partie que il leur pleust avoir pitié de soy[127] et de sa fille morte et que il leur pleust avant oïr les prieres de trois tribuns amis de Virginie que de la gent claudyenne, qui avoit volu usurper royaume dessur eulz, et que, aussi comme cil tribun estoient créé a l'aide du plebe,[128] aussi requeroient il que li plebes[129] en cestuy cas leur voeillent aidier. Si semblerent les lermes de Virginius estre plus justes que celles de Claudius. Et pour ce, perdue toute esperance d'eschaper, tout avant que venist le jour de son jugement, Appius Claudius a hasté et pourchascié sa mort. **(par. 10)** Aprez la mort Appius Claudius, li tribuns Munitorius a mises mainz en Spurius Oppius por ce que il estoit en la cité quant Appius, ses compainz, juga les injustes vindices contre Virginie, et ne mist nule painne pour l'empeeschier. Mais encore plus nuysoit au dit Oppius une autre injure que il avoit fait que celle que il n'avoit pas empeeschiee, quar contre lui fu produits uns tesmoings, qui vint et sept fois avoit esté aus gages en chevalerie, et plusieurs fois, par ses merites, avoit esté guerredonnez extraordinairement, et aportoit les dons a luy fais en la presence du pueple, li quelz rompi sa robe et moustra son dos devant touz qui estoit touz despeciez de verges par le dit Spurius; et ne requeroit autre chose, mes que se li diz Spurius pouoit alleguer une seule coupe pour laquelle il li deust avoir fait telle injure, il voloit que luy, touz privez, se peust derrechief forsener contre luy. Si fu li diz Oppius menez en lienz et illueques, avant le jour de son jugement, fist la fin de sa vie. Si publierent li tribun les biens des dessus diz Oppius et Claudius, et li autre dy home s'en allerent en exil et furent vistement touz leurs bienz publiez, ce est a dire confisquiez au commun. Et ensement Marcus Claudius, qui avoit esté demandeurs de Virginie, fu condempnez, mais Virginius li relascha la painne de la mort, et fu baniz de Rome et s'en alla a Tibur en exil. Et finablement

[125] remirez *O*; corr. *G*
[126] pueple *O*; corr. *JG*
[127] lui *O*; corr. *GJ*
[128] pueple *O*; corr. *GJ*
[129] pueples *O*; corr. *GJ*

moment lie fettered and chained among diurnal and nocturnal thieves. Out of grace, lords, turn your thoughts away from wrath for a bit and toward understanding and reflection, and sooner consider giving this man alone to the many Claudians who implore you on his behalf than refusing the prayers of so many worthy men out of hatred for him alone; and do this grace not for him but for the Claudian name and his lineage. I implore this of you for my son," he said, "not because he has returned to my good graces, but because I wish to rescue him, as far as I am able, from adverse fortune. Surely," he said, "since you have recovered liberty through power and force, it is reasonable for you to strengthen it through clemency and the concord of the orders." **(par. 9)** There were some of those who were moved by the words of the old man Claudius, more out of pity for him than for the man whose cause he pleaded. But on the other hand, Verginius implored the plebs that they choose to have pity on him and on his dead daughter and to heed the prayers of the three tribune allies of Verginia[97] before those of the Claudian clan, which had wished to impose royalty upon them; and that just as these tribunes had been elected with the assistance of the plebs, so they implored that the plebs should assist them in this matter. Thus, the tears of Verginius seemed more just than those of [Gaius] Claudius. For this reason, all hope of escape having been lost, Appius Claudius hastened and pursued his own death even before the day of his judgment had come. **(par. 10)** After the death of Appius Claudius, the tribune Munitorius [Numitorius] arrested Spurius Oppius, as he was in the city when Appius, his comrade, pronounced judgment against Verginia according to the unjust vindices, and as he took no pains to prevent it. Yet another wrongful act was even more damaging to said Oppius, one he had committed rather than the one he had not prevented; for a witness was produced against him, one who had been in knightly service twenty-seven times, and who had many times received extraordinary citations for his merits; and he bore before the people the awards given to him, tearing open his robes and showing everyone his back, which had been entirely mutilated by rods at the order of said Spurius; and he called for nothing, provided that if said Spurius could claim a single misdeed for which he ought to have caused him such an injury, he wished that he [Spurius], albeit no longer a public official, might take his rage out on him once again. Thus, said Oppius was led off in fetters and subsequently brought an end to his own life before the day of his judgment. Then, the tribunes made public property of the goods of the aforementioned Oppius and [Appius] Claudius, and the other decemvirs went into exile and all their goods were swiftly made public property, meaning they were confiscated by the commons. Likewise, Marcus Claudius, who had been the claimant against Verginia, was condemned; yet Verginius set aside the death penalty for him, and he was banished from Rome and went into exile at Tibur. Finally,

[f. 57vc] les manez, ce sont les esperites de la pucele, furent plus bon euré le morte que le vive,[130] si que, aprez ce que il eussent couru par pluseurs nobles maisons demandans painnes et venjances, puniz touz les coulpables, il se sont reposé.

---

[130] *O* has "que le vive," which could also be read as "qu'ele vive"; qu'elle vive *J*; lui m. que elle v. *G.*

the manes, which are the maiden's spirits, were happier with her dead rather than that she might have lived, such that after they had run through several noble houses demanding penalties and reprisals, and with all the guilty punished, they took their rest.

NOTES TO THE TRANSLATION

[1] In general, we have indicated differences between Livy's text and Bersuire's in the translation rather than the edition, where the notes are limited to the signaling of variants and occasions when the control manuscripts were preferred to the base manuscript. Unless otherwise indicated, we cite Livy in the Loeb edition and translation: *Livy in Fourteen Volumes*, trans. B. O. Foster, vol. 2 (Books 3 and 4) (1922; Cambridge, MA: Loeb Classical Library, Harvard University Press, 1967), pp. 143–99.

[2] As Kathryn Gravdal argues in *Ravishing Maidens: Writing Rape in Medieval French Literature and* Law (Philadelphia: University of Pennsylvania Press, 1991), the medieval language of rape is notoriously ambiguous, relying heavily on "periphrasis, metaphor, and slippery lexematic exchanges" (p. 2). The word "stupre" refers to illicit intercourse of any kind, consensual or forced, or more generally to dishonor, disgrace, or defilement. As Lucretia is unquestionably raped, we have not hesitated to use that word. For the various threats against Verginia's chastity, we have been more cautious and have indicated the ambiguities of Bersuire's (and Livy's) language in the notes.

[3] Bersuire's translation of Livy features an alphabetical glossary of Roman terms that had no equivalent in fourteenth-century French. We occasionally cite the glossary, as edited from the Rawlinson manuscript by Marie-Hélène Tesnière in "À propos de la traduction de Tite-Live par Pierre Bersuire: Le *manuscrit Oxford, Bibliothèque Bodléienne, Rawlinson C447*," *Romania* 118/471–72 (2000): 449–98. The glossary contains the following entry for "decemvir" and "decemviratus":

> C'estoit un office fait par accident qui est appelés en latin *decemviratus*, et chascun avoit non *decemvir* ou *triumvir* ou *duumvir*. Et ce estoit quant pour faire aucun fait notable on eslisoit dix hommes ou deuz ou troiz, auquel on donoit plain pooir de celi besoingne faire, si comme fu quant les loys furent aporteez d'Athenez, car lors on esliut "diz hommes" pour lez publier et pour i ajouster .II. Tables. Et ceulz je appelé "dyhommez" en plurer, et chascun par soi appele je "dyhomme," car autre françois je ne li puis doner. Et aussi trouveras "terhomme" et "duyhomme," [. . .] *triumvir* et *duumvir*. [Tesnière 492]

This was an office created in ad hoc situations and called, in Latin, *decem-viratus*; and each man who occupied it was called a *decemvir* (or *triumvir* or *duumvir*). This was because, when [the Romans] wanted to accomplish a notable deed, they elected ten men (or two or three) to whom they gave full power to fulfill that need. This is how it happened when the laws were brought from Athens; for at that time, they elected decemvirs to promulgate them [the first ten tables] and to add two tables. I call these men "dy-hommez" in the plural, and I call each on his own "dyhomme," for I can assign them no other French word. You will also find "terhomme" and "duy-homme" for *triumvir* and *duumvir*.

Bersuire is referring to the Laws of the Twelve Tables, which were based on Athenian law, specifically the Solonian Constitution. The first ten of the Twelve Tables were drafted by the original decemvirate, while a second decemvirate drafted the last two tables. The first decemvirate was held to be fair and just, while the second swiftly became tyrannical, using the last two tables to impose harsh restrictions on the plebs. Appius was a member of both decemvirates. He was appointed to the first and, according to Livy, rigged the election for the second to ensure that he would be able to dominate it easily. See *History of Rome* 3.35–38.

4   Our base manuscript, Oxford, Bodleian Library, Rawlinson C 447 (*O*), reads "verge du pueple," though both context and Livy's source text dictate "verge du plebe," which is the reading found in Sainte Geneviève 777 (*G*) and Bibliothèque nationale de France, nafr. 27401 (*J*). The scribe makes the same error repeatedly in the Verginius-Verginia story. Bersuire himself distinguishes carefully between "peuple" and "plebe" and supplies an entry for them in the glossary, which is found in the Rawlinson manuscript but was copied in a different hand:

> "Peuple" et "plebe" avoit tele différence, car "peuple" romain emportoit tout, c'est a dire noblez et non noblez; "plebe" emportoit seulement lez bas et les petit et le commun. Si que li noble estoient appelé "pere" et "patricien," li non noble estoient appelé "plebe," et tous ensamble "peuple." [Tesnière 496]

> "Peuple" and "plebe" differed in this way: the Roman "peuple" included everyone, that is nobles and nonnobles; "plebe" included only the low, the little, and the common. While the nobles were called "pere" and "patricien," the nonnobles were called "plebe," and both together were called "peuple."

We have emended our text to conform to Bersuire's distinction.

5   Bersuire tends to follow Livy in abbreviating or omitting first names. He also sometimes gives inaccurate versions of family or clan names. We have emended our translation to include full, accurate proper names, adopting the spellings used in the Loeb and placing missing elements or corrections in brackets.

6   Algidum was an ancient city at the foot of Mount Algidus on the Via Latina.

7   Bersuire adds a reference to "chevaliers" here, whereas Livy indicates only that Verginius served well in the army: "vir exempli recti domi militiaeque" ("a man of exemplary life at home and in the army"; 3.44.2). In ancient Rome, Verginius would not have been an *eques* ("knight"), as the *equites* were an elite class, ranked just below the senators. Bersuire elsewhere renders *milites* ("soldiers") as *chevaliers* ("knights"), *commilites* ("fellow soldiers") as *compaingnons chevaliers* ("comrade knights"), and *militia* ("army") as *chevalerie* ("knightly troops"). We have preserved Bersuire's nomenclature even when it misrepresents Roman social distinctions.

8   Livy uses the word *liberi*, a *plurale tantum* that derives from *liber*, "free, as opposed to enslaved," and that refers to progeny in general, regardless of number and, often, gender. Here and elsewhere, Bersuire adheres to Livy, rendering *liberi* as the plural "enfants." It is unclear, however, how many children Verginius had. Icilius will later refer to Verginia as Verginius's "unica filia" ("only daughter"), and some readers (including Chaucer's Physician, who may have been influenced by the story of Jephthah in Judges 11) have taken this to mean that Verginius had only one child.

9   Lucius Icilius was elected Tribune of the Plebs in 456 BCE. He was known for setting aside public lands on the Aventine Hill for plebeian residences.

10   Bersuire translates Livy's *cliens* as "sergent," which typically denotes a servant (from Latin *servire*, "to serve"). However, as R. M. Ogilvie notes, in *A Commentary on Livy: Books 1–5* (Oxford: Clarendon Press, 1965), Claudius was a client to his patron Appius, was likely descended from "one of the Claudian *clientes* mentioned in [*History of Rome*] 2.16.4" (p. 480), and was hardly a servant. The patron-client relationship involved mutual obligations: while the patron was obligated "to protect his client's interests at law…and to safeguard his livelihood," the client was in turn obligated "to follow his patron to war…, to come to his aid in financial straits…, and to support him in political campaigns" (p. 480).

11   Marcus Claudius bears Appius's name as he was a client of the Claudian clan. Ogilvie speculates that Marcus was "a freedman or the descendant of one" (p. 479), meaning that Appius "retained a high degree of coercive power over [him]" (p. 480).

12   Bersuire departs here from the *Ab urbe condita*, in which Appius instructs Claudius "to claim the girl as his slave, and not to yield to those who demanded her liberation [secundum libertatem…vindicias], thinking that the absence

of the maiden's father afforded an opportunity for the wrong" (3.44.5). "La loi des vindices" (or, later, simply "les vindices") is Bersuire's translation of *vindiciae*: a set of laws that were enshrined in the Twelve Tables and that applied to disputes over the rightful owner of a piece of property, whether an object, a plot of land, or an enslaved person. *Vindiciae* derives from *vindico*, which in legal usage refers to two different procedures: *vindicare in servitutem*, "to assert one's title to, claim as one's property (what is in the possession of another)," and *vindicare in libertatem*, "to claim as free (one who asserts he is wrongly held in slavery)." See *Oxford Latin Dictionary*, ed. P. G. W. Glare, corr. edn. (Oxford: Clarendon Press, 1996), s.v., "uindico." Appius is anxious to avoid the invocation of the latter procedure, as Roman law stipulated that at the initial hearing in a *causa liberalis*, courts must presume in favor of liberty when the property under dispute is a human being. See Ogilvie, *Commentary*, p. 482. Bersuire neglects to specify what kind of vindices Appius did not want to allow and what he had in mind with his plan. He also attributes reflection on the absence of Verginius to Claudius (see par. 5, below) rather than to Appius.

13 This marginal note is one of two in the Verginia episode, both pertaining to the vindices. The second appears during Appius's trial, toward the end of the episode. The first marginal note refers to *vindicare in libertatem* only, while the second refers to both *vindicare in libertatem* and *in servitutem* (see note 12, above). In both marginal notes, *vindices* is offered as a translation for the Latin *vindicta*, a legal ritual that Livy does not depict but that is related to *vindiciae*. As part of this ritual, opposing parties laid competing claims to a piece of property by touching it with a rod called either *festuca* ("stalk or stem") or *vindicta*. The legal citation in this marginal note is to Pomponius's *Enchiridion*, as it was incorporated into the *Digest of Justinian* 1.2, "De origine iuris et omnium magistratuum et successione prudentium" ("On the Origin of Law and of the Different Magistracies as well as the Succession of Those Learned in the Law"). Pomponius explains that Appius himself inserted the vindices into the Twelve Tables and adds that the law was established at least since the time of Lucius Junius Brutus, who "allowed interim liberty in the case of Vindex, the slave of the Vitellii, whose information had brought to light a treasonable conspiracy [by Brutus's own sons]." According to Livy, Vindex (also known as Vindicius) was the first slave to receive manumission through the touch of the *vindicta* and lent his name to the ritual (2.5). Scholars dismiss this claim as spurious.

14 Ogilvie notes that the first Roman school was established later (in 234 BCE), that Roman children were educated at home, and that Livy (or his source) likely invented these schools as pretext for placing Verginia at the forum (pp. 480–81).

15 The action of laying on the hand ("manus iniectio") was one of the steps in calling a defendant to justice. According to Ogilvie, the correct procedure begins with a verbal call to justice ("in ius vocatio"), and the hand is involved

only if the defendant refuses to appear before a judge. The brutish Marcus Claudius has reversed the order and swiftly moves to threatening force, distorting "manus iniectio," which is "a stage in a legal action, not an act of violence" (p. 481). Bersuire incorrectly attributes lust to Claudius, who is, for Livy, merely "the minister of the decemvir's lust" (3.44.6). See note 19, below.

[16] *Quirites* is "a name given to the citizens of Rome collectively in their peacetime functions (esp. in solemn addresses and appeals)." See *Oxford Latin Dictionary*, s.v., "Quirites." Livy mentions the "Quiritium" only (3.44.7). Bersuire adds the reference to the "pueple romain."

[17] Bersuire alters Livy's text, conflating two distinct groups who responded to the attack on Verginia: those who knew Verginius and Icilius and were compelled to help out of love for them; and "the crowd," which "was influenced by the shamelessness of the attempt" (3.44.8).

[18] The verb "efforcer" is often used to signify "rape" in medieval French texts, though it can also mean "to constrain or use force against someone."

[19] Bersuire misses the force of Livy's text, which, for Ogilvie, "reiterates the procedure of *in ius vocatio* and *manus iniectio*. Claudius invites the girl to come with him to the praetor. When she declines he invokes the crowd as witnesses to the invitation conveyed by the *manus iniectio* and to testify that she should follow him to the tribunal" (p. 482). See note 15, above.

[20] Livy refers to Numitorius as Verginia's "avus" (3.45.4), which can be translated in various ways including "grandfather" and "great-uncle." Translators often prefer the latter, as it helps explain a subsequent reference to Numitorius as Verginia's "avunculus," meaning "uncle" or "great-uncle" (3.54.11). Bersuire may have wished to preserve the ambiguity, as he translates "avus" as "aeulz," meaning "grandfather" or "forebear." However, in the later passage (see note 75, below), he names Numitorius, along with two other men, as "oncles" to Verginius rather than Verginia. To add to the confusion, the *O* scribe gives "Munitorius" both here and in two subsequent passages (see Chs. 30 and 33), while the *J* scribe corrects to "Numitorius" here but not in the later passages.

[21] "Violer" can be taken as "to do violence or damage," "to break or violate," or "to rape."

[22] First mentioned in Livy 2.8, *provocatio* refers to the right to appeal the coercive or procedural actions of a magistrate directly to the Roman people. It was understood to place democratic limitations on the power of the magistracy and was, according to Ogilvie, "the end-product of long evolution," starting with "the creation of the tribunate and the provisions of the Twelve Tables and of the Valerio-Horatian laws" (p. 252). The Valerio-Horatian laws are presented below.

23 As Gravdal notes, "fame esforcer" (or, as here, "faire force") is "the most frequent medieval locution for rape" (p. 3) and is defined as such by the thirteenth-century jurist Philippe de Beaumanoir. Its semantic field is quite large, however, and includes both legitimate and illegitimate uses of force.

24 Like the Latin *fides*, "foy" signifies the qualities that give an individual a good name: honesty, honor, sincerity, loyalty, etc.

25 When the law of the vindices was invoked, the party who took possession of the disputed property or person was obliged to pledge sureties to guarantee subsequent appearances in court.

26 Father and daughter have donned the garb of woe, which signifies affliction and mourning through the neglect of personal appearance. Initially, the cause is a public, legal calamity, though it will become a personal one when Verginius decides to kill his daughter.

27 This is the shrine of Venus Cloacina, associated both with the Cloaca Maxima (Rome's first sewer, which passed through the forum) and, in Pliny's *Natural History*, with rites of purification (*cluere*, "to purify"). The implication, which is borne out by Verginius's subsequent speech to Appius, is that Verginia's death is a blood sacrifice that will cleanse and renew the city.

28 Livy's text reads "ab lanio cultro" ("a knife from a butcher"; 3.48.5), which Bersuire seems to have misconstrued as "alban[i]o cultro" ("Albanian knife").

29 Bersuire echoes the law of the vindices with the verbs *vendiquier* ("to claim") and *revendiquier* ("to reclaim").

30 Livy uses the term *caput* ("head"; 3.48.5), which Bersuire translates as *chief*. While both *caput* and *chief* carry the figurative meaning of "a chief person or leader," Middle French lacks the tropological extension to "physical life" that is found in Latin. Here as elsewhere, Bersuire gives the French form of a Latin word but maintains one of the meanings in Latin that does not come into Middle French.

31 In his glossary, Bersuire notes that the Roman nobility are alternately called fathers and patricians (see note 4, above, and Tesnière 496). In the Verginius-Verginia story, he tends to translate "patres" as "pers" and "patricii" as "patriciens," reserving "pere" for a biological father. We have translated both "pers" and "patriciens" as "patricians," though we have noted instances in which Livy and/or Bersuire seem to intend something different, notably a reference to members of the Senate or to Rome's forefathers. Although Bersuire discusses the term "senateur" in his glossary (Tesnière 497), he does not use it in the Verginius-Verginia story.

32 Lucius Valerius Poplicola Potitus and Marcus Horatius Barbatus were Roman patricians and senators who openly criticized the second decemvirate out of sympathy with the plebs. The Valerio-Horatian laws, which are presented below, are often attributed to them.

33   In Livy, Valerius and Horatius make no mention of reason, referring only to a legal course of action: "si iure ageret" (3.49.3).

34   In Livy, the subject of this clause is Valerius and Horatius, who seek to protect Icilius from Appius (3.49.3).

35   Following Livy, Bersuire distinguishes between a *personne privée*, an ordinary citizen, and a *personne publique*, a person invested with an official state function. The suggestion is that by refusing to relinquish the role of decemvir, which was intended as a temporary, ad hoc appointment, Appius has unlawfully usurped public office.

36   Bersuire omits a sentence that immediately follows this one in Livy: "Hinc atrox rixa oritur" ("This led to a desperate struggle"; 3.49.4).

37   The fasces were bundles of wooden rods bound together to suggest the collective power of the state and the authority of the magistracy. They were often borne by lictors and were fitted with axes, which served both as weapons and as symbols of capital punishment.

38   Spurius Oppius Cornicen was a plebeian member of the second decemvirate and one of Appius's close allies.

39   This location is not otherwise attested in Livy or elsewhere. Ogilvie cites a claim that it may have been "one of the peaks or spurs of the Algidus range," approximately twelve miles southeast of Rome.

40   Bersuire uses "tentes" as a synecdoche for a military encampment, occasionally (though not here) as a translation for *castra* or "camp."

41   Togas were worn in the city, and the suggestion is that many of the people present in the camp were dressed as civilians. Bersuire defines *toga* for his readers, associating it (somewhat paradoxically, given its usage here) with peace: "'Togue' estoit aucune robe honeste de quoi li Romain usoient en tamps de pays" ("'Toga' was a sort of honorable dress that the Romans used in times of peace"; Tesnière 497).

42   Following Livy, Bersuire uses the word "stupre," which is also how he described the fate of Lucretia (see note 2, above).

43   Bersuire omits a clause: "The decemvirs, troubled alike by what they saw and by what they heard had taken place in Rome" (3.50.12).

44   Livy uses a different kind of antithesis: "And so long as they mildly remonstrated, they got no answer; but if one of them tried to use his authority, they told him that they were men, and armed" (3.50.12–13).

45   The Aventine Hill is positioned outside the pomerium, an ancient sacred boundary that surrounded the city of Rome. Everything outside the pomerium was understood as territory belonging to Rome but not properly a part of the city. Because of its marginal status, the Aventine was associated with plebeian jurisdiction and revolt.

⁴⁶   In Livy, this is the same Spurius Oppius Cornicen who offers aid to Appius in the forum and who is arrested and imprisoned after him. See Chs. 26 and 33.

⁴⁷   Spurius Tarpeius was a member of a minor patrician family; Gaius Julius was a member of the first decemvirate; and according to Livy, Publius Sulpicius was one of the Roman commissioners sent to Athens to make a copy of the Solonian Constitution (3.31.8).

⁴⁸   Bersuire refers to "la chose publique" here, translating Livy's "rei [publicae]." Bersuire's glossary offers the following definition:

> Chose publique n'est autre chose mes que l'estat publique ou le commun, et est nom general a tous estas de terres, pays, royaumes et cites ou quelconques autres communautés de gens. Mes quant par especial on veut parler de l'estat d'une cité ou d'un royaume, lors dist on la "chose romaine" et la "chose carthageyse." [Tesnière 489]

> *Chose publique* is nothing other than the public or common [i.e., third] estate, and it is also a general name for all the estates of lands, countries, kingdoms, and cities, or of any other such communities of people. Yet when one wishes to speak specifically of the estate of a city or of a kingdom, one speaks then of the "Roman *chose*" and of the "Carthaginian *chose*."

⁴⁹   The *tribuni militum*, or "tribunes of the soldiers," were consular tribunes who were elected in place of consuls and functioned as magistrates. In Livy, their election often functions as a political tactic in the conflicts between plebeians and patricians.

⁵⁰   Livy's original is "filia inulta" ("unavenged daughter"; 3.51.4), which Bersuire seems to have read as "filia unica," echoing Icilius's reference, above, to Verginius's "only daughter." Given (a) that "inulta" and "unica" would have started with five minims and that the minims could each be read as "i," "m," "n," or "u"; and (b) that the "c" and "t" can, depending upon the scribe, appear very similar (especially in a sequence of letters), the one word could easily have been taken for the other, especially if the "i" had been dropped in the model being translated by Bersuire.

⁵¹   The Sabines were an ancient Italic tribe whose territory lay to the northeast of Rome.

⁵²   Lucius Siccius, whose story immediately precedes that of Verginius and Verginia (3.43), was a decorated warrior, plebeian tribune, and champion in the struggle against the patricians. During Rome's campaign against the Sabines, he began to promote secession among the troops and was assassinated by a company of his own soldiers. The army suspected the involvement of the decemvirs, who tried to cover their tracks by burying Siccius with military honors at state expense.

⁵³   Livy: "Men's anger on being reminded of the murder of Siccius [was] no less violent than that which was kindled in them by the new story of the maiden whose dishonour had been so foully sought" (3.51.7–8).

⁵⁴   Bersuire uses the term "comice" and offers the following definition in his glossary:

> Sachiés car li Romain changierent chascun an tous leur magistras et offici-ers publiques fussent consul, preteur, edile ou autres, et lessoient les vielz et eslisoient novels. Sachiés donques car le liu ou l'election des novelz mag-istras et officiers se fesoit chascun an estoit appelé "comice" en singuler, et le fait et l'estat des dictes elections estoit appelés les "comices" en plurer, si comme tu trouveras que mout de fois on fait mencion des "comices consu-laires," "pretoriaus" ou "tribunaires." [Tesnière 489–99]

> Know that every year the Romans changed their magistrates and public officers, be they consul, praetor, aedile, or others, and let go of the old and elected the new. Know, then, that the place where the election of the new magistrates and officers took place each year was called "comice" in the singular, and that the conduct and outcome of said elections was called "comices" in the plural, such that you will often find mention of "consular," "praetorian," or "tribunal comices."

⁵⁵   The Colline Gate was situated at the north end of the Servian Wall, an ancient defensive barrier built around the city.

⁵⁶   Marcus Oppius is not otherwise known to historians, and Sextus Manilius is likely an invention (Ogilvie p. 491).

⁵⁷   The final clause of this sentence is not found in Livy.

⁵⁸   Bersuire misses a clause from Livy: "Decemviri querentes se in ordinem cogi" ("The decemvirs, complaining that they were being deprived of their office"; 3.51.13).

⁵⁹   Marcus Duillius was elected tribune in 470 BCE and was said to have served with distinction. According to Livy, he never failed to support the plebs in their struggles with the decemvirs (3.54).

⁶⁰   The Sacred Mount (*Mons Sacer*) is a hill outside the ancient boundaries of Rome. It was used as a site for sacred rituals and divinations, though its name is attributed to the Lex Sacrata, a law (or, more properly, an oath) ratified in 494 BCE to end the First Plebeian Secession (see Livy 2.32–33). The Lex Sacrata made plebeian tribunes personally sacrosanct, so that anyone who harmed them was subject to the death penalty. It also made plebeians a sworn confederacy, united against the patricians.

61   The Via Nomentana, originally known as the Via Ficulensis because it led from the Colline Gate to the village of Ficulea, was eventually extended to Nomentum, modern Mentana, about fourteen miles northeast of Rome.

62   Ogilvie (p. 492, referring to Livy 2.32.4) sees this as a reference to the First Secession, which ended when a Senate envoy of plebeian descent, Agrippa Menenius Lanatus, used the fable of the belly and its members to convince the plebs to negotiate a treaty. The treaty was ratified without further threat of violence. Bersuire uses the word "pers" here, though the reference is to the forefathers of the plebs rather than to the patrician class.

63   "Patres conscripti" is a collective title used to address Roman senators as a body.

64   Bersuire adds the negative. Livy: "Is it to roofs and walls you will render judgment?" (3.52.7).

65   Livy's text reads "plebem" here, though mss. *O*, *G*, and *J* all give a form of "peuple."

66   Livy: "And it was Icilius too who, when terms were discussed and the commissioners inquired what the plebeians demanded, made such requests, in pursuance of an understanding already reached before the arrival of the envoys, that it was apparent they based their hope more on equity than on arms" (3.53.3–4).

67   There are significant departures from the original throughout this section of the translation. Here, Livy's text reads: "For the recovery of the tribunician power and the appeal were the things they sought – things which had been the help of the plebs before the election of decemvirs; – and that it should not be held against any man that he had incited the soldiers or the people to recover their liberties by secession. Only in regard to the punishment of the decemvirs was their demand a harsh one; for they thought it just that the decemvirs should be delivered up to them, and threatened to burn them alive" (3.53.4–6).

68   Livy: "To these proposals the commissioners replied: 'The demands which have been prompted by your judgment are so right that they ought to have been accorded you voluntarily; for you seek in them guarantees of liberty, not of a licence to make attacks on others. But your anger calls for pardon rather than indulgence, seeing that hatred of cruelty is driving you headlong into cruelty, and almost before you are free yourselves you are wishing to lord it over your adversaries'" (3.53.6–8).

69   Livy: "Will the time never come when our state shall rest from punishments visited either by the patricians on the Roman plebs or by the plebs on the patricians? A shield is what you need more than a sword. It is enough and more than enough for a lowly citizen when he lives in the enjoyment of equal rights in the state, neither inflicting an injury nor receiving one" (3.53.8–9).

70 Bersuire misses an especially colorful sentence that immediately follows this one in Livy: "Dandus invidiae est sanguis" ("Hatred must have its offering of blood"; 3.54.4).

71 Livy: "I too am willing to relinquish [or more literally, not even I will delay giving up] the decemvirate" (3.54.4).

72 Livy refers to Quintus as "pontifex maximus" (3.54.5), suggesting that Rome had a college of high priests and that its leader presided over the tribune elections of 450 BCE – perhaps, as Cicero surmises in *Pro Cornelio*, because there was no magistrate to do so. Ogilvie argues that this was historically improbable, as the tribunate was not recognized as part of the Roman constitution until the Valerio-Horatian laws were passed a year later (pp. 494–95).

73 Bersuire seems to have missed the sense of Livy's "fraudi" (3.54.5), which signifies "a cause for punishment." The Old French word "fraude" does not have this meaning.

74 Livy indicates "tribunes of the plebs" (3.54.11), though the three manuscripts we consulted all give "tribuns de pueple."

75 In Livy, only one of these men is named as a relative: Publius Numitorius is Verginia's "avunculus," meaning "uncle" or "great-uncle" (3.54.11). Bersuire describes all three men as uncles to Verginius rather than to Verginia. For more detail, see note 20, above.

76 Bersuire misreads Livy, who indicates that "these matters were all transacted by the council of the plebs" (3.54.15) and makes no mention of Gaius Flaminius, who lived in a later period (ca. 275–217 BCE) and was a plebeian, not a patrician.

77 Built in 221 BCE, the Flaminian Circus was strongly associated with the plebs, who held the Ludi Plebeii there.

78 This chapter describes the Valerio-Horatian laws. The three main laws are *plebiscite*, which made the resolutions of the Plebeian Council binding to all Romans; *provocatio*, which restored the right of appeal to the people; and *sacrosanctitas*, which restored the powers of the plebeian tribunes and made them inviolable according to sacred law.

79 Bersuire seems to have added the date, which does not appear in Livy.

80 Bersuire's glossary features an entry for this term:

> "Plebiscite" estoit appelé aucun establissement que le menu plebe faisoit en sa court par sez tribuns et par ses ediles et par sez magistraz. Car cesti plebe avoit sa court et sez juges tout a port par soy. Et ses juges il appeloient "tribuns plebeyens." [Tesnière 496]

> "Plebiscite" was the name for any ruling that the lowly plebs issued in their court through their tribunes and through their aediles and through their magistrates. For these plebs had their court and their judges entirely at their disposal. And they called their judges "plebeian tribunes."

In reality, the plebiscites were not made by a court but by the assembly of the plebs.

81   The centuriated assembly (*centuriata comitia*) was one of Rome's three voting assemblies. It divided the citizenry into groups of one hundred men, organized by military status and eventually by social class. Gathered as an assembly, these "centuries" were tasked with various legislative, electoral, and judicial functions, with each century receiving one vote.

82   The final clause of this sentence does not appear in Livy.

83   Aediles originally served as assistants to the plebs, performing ad hoc ministerial roles and protecting plebeian access to the Temple of Ceres (*aedis* means "temple" or "shrine"). Bersuire gives an entry for the aediles in his glossary, distinguishing between plebeian and curule aediles (Tesnière 493). The latter role was created in 367 BCE (see Livy 6.42).

84   As Ogilvie notes, scholars have often taken this as a reference to the *decemviri stlitibus iudicandis*, "a panel who were mainly concerned with *causae liberales*." Since Verginia's case is precisely a case involving liberty, "the identification was appropriate enough." However, the decemvir panel was created centuries later, after 242 BCE, and "comprised both patricians and plebeians." Ogilvie concludes that this must therefore be a reference to "one or two plebeian officials of whom we know nothing" (p. 501).

85   Ogilvie offers the following explanation of *sacrosanctitas*: "When a man committed an *iniuria* against another man his *iniuria* surrendered him into the power of the other man. So when a man committed an offence against a god either by violating a god's sanctuary or, as here, by breaking an oath made in a god's name, he became forfeit to that god – *sacer*. The only way in which a god could claim this man was by death which was not in any sense a sacrifice but the speedy delivery of the offender to his master," with "the one who dispatched the offender . . . exempt from the ordinary penalties and taboos connected with causing death" (p. 500). In this instance, the god to whom forfeit is owed is Ceres, the central deity of the Aventine Triad, which also included Liber and Libera, gods of wine, fertility, and freedom. All three deities were associated with the plebs and were worshiped on the Aventine Hill. The festival of Liber and Libera, known as Liberalia, was associated with freedom of speech and other rights.

86   Bersuire considerably condenses Livy's discussion of *sacrosanctitas*, which distinguishes between tribunes, who were made sacrosanct at the time their office (and that of the aediles) was created, and aediles, who could only become sacrosanct by suing a higher magistrate.

87   The *senatus consulta* were opinions decreed by the Roman Senate regarding laws presented by a consul or praetor. The opinions were officially held to be advisory, though magistrates often treated them as if they were legally binding.

88   See note 13, above.

89   We have preserved Livy's word choice here, for lack of a reasonable English equivalent. The *viatores* were one of four classes of *apparitores*: civil servants charged with assisting the magistrates in their work, whether as notaries (*scribae*), lictors (*lictores*), heralds (*praecones*), or summoners (*viatores*). The *viatores* were so named because they regularly traveled the streets and highways. The equivalent Bersuire finds in French is "sergens voiers," an officer entrusted with policing public streets.

90   Livy's text indicates "plebem," though the three manuscripts we consulted indicate "pueple."

91   Livy's text reads "tribunos plebei" ("tribunes of the plebs"; 3.56.11).

92   According to Ogilvie, Verginius invents the claim that Appius had a prison built. This was "a familiar and savage jibe," encountered in Cicero and even older authors (p. 506).

93   The Latins and Hernici were ancient Italic tribes whose territories lay to the south and southeast of Rome.

94   The Capitoline Hill was the site of the Temple of Jupiter Optimus Maximus, and the word *Capitolium* originally referred to the temple itself.

95   Like the Sabines, the Aequi were an ancient Italic tribe whose territory lay to the east of Rome. Ogilvie notes that there is an apparent inconsistency here, given the preceding reference to war with the Volsci, not the Sabines. He explains that Livy "has compressed to the point of obscurity" (pp. 506–07), as there were in fact two wars ongoing: one with the Sabines and another with the Aequi and Volsci, who had joined forces and therefore represented a single enemy.

96   Livy names Gaius (or Caius) Claudius as Appius's uncle (3.8.1), though according to Ogilvie (p. 423) he was also known as the decemvir's brother. Bersuire seems to have invented the notion that Gaius was Appius's father.

97   The reference seems to be to the "authors of the sedition" mentioned above.

Figure 3 Verginia is called before Appius, *Tite-Live*. A privately held Lillois manuscript, ca. 1470, f. 97v. Courtesy Dr. Jörn Günther Rare Books, Basel (Switzerland).

Figure 4 Icilius attempts to defend Verginia, and a messenger is dispatched to find Verginius. A privately held Lillois manuscript, ca. 1470, f. 98v. Courtesy Dr. Jörn Günther Rare Books, Basel (Switzerland).

Figure 5 Verginius and Verginia appear before Appius to hear Verginia's sentence. A privately held Lillois manuscript, ca. 1470, f. 99r. Courtesy Dr. Jörn Günther Rare Books, Basel (Switzerland).

Figure 6 Verginius kills Verginia with a knife, *Tite-Live*. A privately held Lillois manuscript, ca. 1470, f. 99v. Courtesy Dr. Jörn Günther Rare Books, Basel (Switzerland).

Figure 7 Verginius returns to the army to explain his daughter's fate. A privately held Lillois manuscript, ca. 1470, f. 100r. Courtesy Dr. Jörn Günther Rare Books, Basel (Switzerland).

Figure 8 Appius is forced to answer to Verginius for his crimes, *Tite-Live*. A privately held Lillois manuscript, ca. 1470, f. 104r. Courtesy Dr. Jörn Günther Rare Books, Basel (Switzerland).

Figure 9 Appius is carried off to prison, *Tite-Live*. A privately held Lillois manuscript, ca. 1470, f. 105r. Courtesy Dr. Jörn Günther Rare Books, Basel (Switzerland).

Figure 10 Appius's father appeals for mercy for his son. A privately held Lillois manuscript, ca. 1470, f. 105v. Courtesy Dr. Jörn Günther Rare Books, Basel (Switzerland).

2

The Tale of Lucretia from Pierre Bersuire's *Tite-Live*

The base manuscript for this edition is Oxford, Bodleian Library, Rawlinson C 447 (*O*). Corrections have been made, and occasional variants provided, with the help of Sainte Geneviève 777 (*G*) and BnF nafr. 27401 (*J*). As we noted in the introduction, the *O* manuscript divides each book into chapters, which are in turn divided into paragraphs. The scribe typically marks chapter divisions with a slightly enlarged initial letter (usually the height of two lines) containing filigree-work, next to which, in the text or in the margin, is a rubricated capital *C* followed by the chapter number in Roman numerals, also rubricated. He marks paragraph divisions with alternating red and blue pilcrows in the text and with marginal, rubricated paragraph numbers that restart with each chapter division, though the new paragraph starting at the beginning of the chapter division is usually not indicated by a marginal "1," and numbering starts with the second paragraph. There are no titles or other forms of decoration. The *J* manuscript, the text of which is closely related to our base manuscript, by and large maintains the same chapter and paragraph divisions, including the use of similar decorated initials for chapter divisions and alternating pilcrows (including gold leaf) for paragraph divisions, but without any numbering. All of the other manuscripts, later than these two, contain a different system of shorter chapters accompanied by chapter titles and numbering, many of which coincide with the older chapter or paragraph divisions of *O* and *J*. The later chapter numbers and titles were added to the *O* manuscript as marginal notes at some point in the late fourteenth or early fifteenth century. We have preserved the dual chapter division of ms. *O* in our edition. The markings original to the *O* manuscript appear in boldface within the text. The later markings appear in italics and are set off from the text as separate paragraphs. As is typical of the different divisions, the entirety of the Lucretia episode, which ends the first book of the first decade, is a single chapter in the older division of mss. *O* and *J*, numbered 31 in *O*, but is divided into three chapters in the later division, numbered 47 to 49.

[f. 19ra]

Comment Sextus le filz du roy Tarquin prist a force Lucrece .xlvii. [Ch. 47]

(**.C. xxxi [Ch. 31]**) (**par. 1**) La cité d'Ardee apartenoit[1] au peuple des Rutiliens, la quele gens estoit a celi tempz et en celi eage habundans en richescez, la quele chose fu cause que li roys Tarquins li a meu guerre, por ce que il, veyans que il estoit vuidiés de richeces pour la magnificence des euvres publiquez, les queles il avoit fait, se vouloit enrichesir et apaysier le peuple par l'esperance de la praye, qui outre la cause de l'orgueil du roy estoit meus encontre lui pour ce que il les avoit lonc[2] temps occupez en offices de fevres[3] et de ouvriers[4] et en euvrez serviles. (**par. 2**) Li Romain se sont assayé se la dicte cité poust estre prise par assaut, mes la ou il virent que po i profitoient il la ont assise et enclose[5] a l'entour. Mez si comme souvent est acoustumé en guerrez qui par sieges se font, la bataille est plus longue que aigre, ceuls de l'ost avoient assez loisir d'aler et de venir, et especialment lez richez homez plus que les chevaliers. (**par. 3**) Dont il avint que lez royaus juvenceaus aucunez foyz pour passer leur anui fesoient leur convis les uns chiez les autres. Si estoient un jour en la tente Sexte Tarquin et avecquez eulz estoit uns nobles hom de Rome qui estoit appelés Collatins Tarquins, filz Eger, qui sopoit avec eulz. Si se esmeut entre euls une question de leur famez, la quelle d'elles estoit plus suffissant. Et come chascuns estrivast et loast la soie merveilleusement, Collatins leur a dit que de ce ne faut ja faire paroles, car assez tost pooit on savoir par fait et par experience que Lucrece sa fame estoit milleur dez autres. "Si," dist il, "nostre juvente a en soi vigour, montons a cheval et alons a Rome soubdeinement por veir que font nos fames, qui ne donent garde, et savrons de chascune en quele present besoingne elle serra trouvee." (**par. 4**) Le conseil Collatin a pleu a chascun et leur sembla milleur pour ce que il l'a fet soubdeinement sans predeliberer. Et pour ce les juvenceaus, qui erent eschaufiez du vin[6], montent sur les chevaus et s'en vont a Rome, eu quel lieu il sont arrivés tout a point, [f. 19rb] a heure de prinsomme, la ou lez tenebres de la nuit commencierent a cloirre. Et d'ilecquez s'en sont alé a Collace a l'oustel Collatin, ou il trovierent Lucrece sa fame non pas en l'estat[7] ou il avoient trouvé lez autres brus royalz, les quelez il avoient trouveez soy esbatanz et passans le tempz avecquez leur compeingnez en convis et en gales. Eincez la trouverent tarde nuit occupee en lanifice, seant en mi la meson entre les chamberieres, qui

[1]   A celui temps appartenoit la cité d'Ardee *G*
[2]   dont *O*; corr. *G*
[3]   fievrez *O*; corr. *G*
[4]   ovrers *O*; corr. *G*
[5]   enclous *OJ*; corr. *G*
[6]   du vin *om. O*; corr. *GJ*
[7]   l'estal *O*; corr. *GJ*

How Sextus, the son of King Tarquin, took Lucretia by force (Ch. 47)[1]

(Ch. 31) (par. 1) The city of Ardea belonged to the Rutulian people,[2] a nation that was at that time and in that age overflowing with wealth, which was the reason why King Tarquin[3] declared war against them; for seeing that he was devoid of wealth on account of the magnificence of the public works he had made, he wished to enrich himself and to appease the people with the hope of booty;[4] the people were stirred up against the king not only because of his pride but also because he had for a long time occupied them with the jobs of craftsmen and laborers and the tasks of slaves.[5] **(par. 2)** The Romans tested their forces to see if said city could be taken by assault; but when they saw they were gaining little advantage that way, they besieged it and surrounded it on all sides. But since, as is often the case with wars conducted by siege, the battle is longer than it is bitter, the men of the army had a good bit of freedom to come and go, especially the wealthy men, less so the knights.[6] **(par. 3)** For this reason, it happened that the royal youths sometimes killed time by holding festive banquets at one another's lodgings. Thus, one day they were in the tent of Sextus Tarquin[7] and with them was a nobleman of Rome who was called Collatine Tarquin [Lucius Tarquinius Collatinus], son of Egerius,[8] and who dined with them. A question then arose among them about their wives, regarding which of them was the worthiest. And as each man entered the dispute and praised his own wife extravagantly, Collatine told them that there was no need to make speeches about it, for it would very soon be possible, by deed and by observation, for them to ascertain that his wife Lucretia was better than the others. "If," he said, "our youthful company has enough vigor in it, let us mount our horses and go right away surreptitiously to Rome to see what our wives are up to; since they are not expecting this, we will find out, about each and every one of them, what private activity they are at present engaged in."[9] **(par. 4)** Collatine's counsel was pleasing to each man and seemed all the better to them because he devised it on the spot, without deliberating ahead of time.[10] And for this reason, the youths, who were heated up with wine, mount their horses and head off to Rome, where they arrived at just the right time, at the first hours of sleep, when the shadows of night began to enclose with their cover. And from there, they went to Collatia,[11] to the home of Collatine, where they found his wife Lucretia not in the state in which they had found the other royal brides, whom they had found enjoying themselves and whiling away the time in feasting and rejoicing with their companions. Quite unlike these women, they found her [Lucretia] toiling late at night at her wool-work,[12] sitting in the middle of her home among the chambermaids, who

veilloient a la besoingne. **(par. 5)** La loenge de l'estrif[8] des dames demoura chez Lucrece, et a esté jugie dez autrez la milleur. Et pour ce son mari, comme celi qui ot eu victoire, convia liement lez juvenceaus royaulz, et furent pour Lucrece[9] benignement[10] receu li Tarquinien dessus dit. Mes pour certain en celui convin, grant[11] ardeur de luxure a pris Sexte Tarquin vers la dicte Lucrece, et se pensa que il l'avroit par force ou autrement, a la quele chose trop forment le aguisoit la beauté et la chasteté de la dicte Lucrece. **(par. 6)** Quant fu de celle foyz[12] lez juvenceaus s'en sont partiz de l'esbat nocturnal et s'en sont revenus a l'ost comme devant. Mez par po de tempz aprés, Sextes Tarquinz, Collatin non savant, avecquez un seul compegnon s'en est venus a Collace, eu quel lieu il a esté courtoisement receus par lez gens Collatin, qui rien ne savoient de sa male entention. Si avint que aprés le souper, la ou on l'ot[13] mené en[14] sa chambre et a son lit, la ou il vit que tous estoient endormis et que entour lui furent assés toutez choses seurez, ardanz et enflammez de l'amour de Lucrece, s'en est alé[15] la ou elle dormoit. Et tenoit en sa dextre[16] son gleve trestout nu, et sa senestre[17] mist sur le piz de la dame, et li a dit ces mos: "Taise toi," dit il, "Lucrece. Voiz ci le gleve nu du quel je t'occirrai, se[18] tu dis un seul[19] mot." **(par. 7)** Comme Lucrece, paoureuse et endormie, veist la mort toute preste et sanz persone qui aidier li peust, et Tarquins d'autre part li requeroit[20] s'amour, et la priast et menaçast[21] et s'esforchast en toutez guisez de l'encliner a soy par feminin[22] courage, finablement il la trouva si forte, sa[23] chasteyé si dure, si hostinee, que par creinte de mort ne[24] la pot encliner. **(par. 8)** Lors a Tarquins a la paour adjousté vergoigne, et li a dit que se elle ne faisoit sa volenté, il ne occirroit la pas[25] seulement mes en outre, avecquez lié morte, il occirroit un garson delés lé.[26] Et ainsi diroit on que il l'avroit occis

---

8   l'estrie *O*; corr. *GJ*
9   Lucree *O*; corr. *GJ*
10 longuement *G*
11 celui qui grant *O*; corr. *G*
12 en cele foys *J*; de celle fois *G*
13 ot *O*; corr. *GJ*
14 en *om. O*; corr. *GJ*
15 alez ale *O*; corr. *J*
16 destre main *G*
17 senestre main *G*
18 se *om. OJ*; corr. *G*
19 sot *J*
20 rejoist *O*; corr. *G*
21 menast *O*; corr. *G*
22 soy le feminin *O*; corr. *G*
23 si *O*; corr. *GJ*
24 na *O*; corr. *GJ*
25 l'ocirroit pas *G*
26 elle *G*

stayed awake because of their task.[13] **(par. 5)** The glory in this competition between ladies remained with Lucretia, and she was judged the best of them. And for this reason, her husband, as he who had claimed victory, extended a warm invitation to the royal youths, and the above-mentioned Tarquinii were kindly received on Lucretia's account. But it is certain that at this revelry, Sextus Tarquin was seized by a great burning lust for said Lucretia, and he thought to himself that he would possess her either by force or otherwise;[14] the beauty and chastity of said Lucretia goaded him toward this deed. **(par. 6)** As he was making this pledge,[15] the youths took their leave from the nocturnal merrymaking and returned as before to the army. Yet not long afterward, Sextus Tarquin, without Collatine's knowledge, returned with a single companion to Collatia, where he was courteously received by Collatine's people, who knew nothing of his evil design. Then it came about that after supper, when they had guided him to his chamber and to his bed, and when he saw that all were asleep and that around him all things were fairly secure, he went, burning and inflamed with love for Lucretia, to the place where she slept. And he held his fully naked sword in his right hand, and he placed his left hand on the lady's breast, and he said these words to her: "Keep silent, Lucretia," he says. "Behold the naked sword with which I will kill you if you say a single word." **(par. 7)** While Lucretia, terrified and drowsy, saw that death was at the ready and that there was no one who could help her, and Tarquin was for his part pleading with her for her love,[16] entreating and threatening her while he strove in every way possible to make himself favorable to her by way of her feminine disposition, ultimately he found her so strong, her chastity so resolute and so obstinate, that he could not win her over even through fear of death. **(par. 8)** Then Tarquin added shame to fear and said to her that if she did not do his bidding, he would not only kill her but in addition, with her dead, he would kill a servant by her side. And thus, people would say that he had killed her

pour ce car il l'avroit trovee[27] avecquez le garson, par dalés lui[28] gisant, et
que elle seroit morte en si vil adultere. **(par. 9)** Ceste vergoigne espoventa[29]
Lucrece si que luxure sourmonta et veinquit chasteté obstinee et que Tarquins
fit de li son plaisir, li quelz, tantost joians et eslevez dont il avoit conquis la
beauté de[30] la dame, s'en est tournez en l'ost.

*Comment Lucrece s'ocist et comment son pere, son mari et ses parens jurerent
sur son sanc .xlviii. [Ch. 48]*

(par. 10) Lucrece fu mout triste de si grant mal que elle avoit fait, si a tantost
un message tremis a Rome a son pere, et d'ilecquez a Ardee a son mari, qui
estoit en l'oust, et leur a mandé que chascun [f. 19vc] de eulz avecquez un
seul et loial compaignon venissent a lé[31] hastivement, car besoing estoit et
que une chose espoentable li estoit avenue. **(par. 11)** Sez perez, qui avoit non
Spurius Lucretius, avecquez un son ami, apelé P. Veler, et ses mariz Collatins
avecquez le dessus dit Junius Brutus, lez quelz deus li messagiers de Lucrece
avoit trouvé a Rome, ou estoient venus par aventure,[32] sont[33] venus a Collace
et trouverent Lucrece, qui par dedenz sa chambre se seoit toute triste. **(par.
12)** Les larmes li soursirent quant elle vit ses amis. Et comme son mari li
demandast se toutes leur choses estoient sauves et bien a point, "Nenil," dist
elle, "pas.[34] Quel chose," dist elle, "peut estre a feme quant elle a perdu sa
chasteté? Ha Collatin," dist elle, "en ton lict sont[35] les entracez[36] d'un home
estrange. Mon corps a esté violé et honi. Mes courages en est innocens, la
mort en serra tesmoing. Mes pour Dieu bailliés moi vos destres et me jurés
voz foys, car[37] li adulterez emportera sa paine. **(par. 13)** Ce est," dit elle,
"Sextus Tarquinius qui est venus a moi, enemis ou lieu d'ouste. Car," dist elle,
"la nuit qui passa il vint a moi tous armez et a tolu a moi – et si a il a soi, se
vouz estez home – toute joie et soulas." **(par. 14)** Lez amis tout par ordre li
ont plevi leur foi et si ont conforté son courage doulent. Et li ont dit que elle
n'i a point pechié[38] puis que elle le fist enforcie, et que la volunté fait le pechié
non paz le corps, et que la ou il n'a point d'assentement il ne peut avoir culpe.
(par. 15) Lors leur a dit Lucrece, "Vous verrés assez tost qu'est ce que on doit

---

27   trouvé trouvé *O*; corr. *GJ*
28   elle *G*
29   espounta *O*; corr. *G*
30   da *O*; corr. *GJ*
31   elle *G*
32   aveture *O*; corr. *GJ*
33   soit *O*; corr. *GJ*
34   il ne le sont pas *G*
35   son *O*; corr. *GJ*
36   ordures *G*
37   que *GJ*
38   pechié *om. OJ*; corr. *G*

for this reason, having found her with the servant, the one lying next to her, and that she had died in an act of vile adultery. **(par. 9)** This shame terrified Lucretia so much that lust overcame and vanquished obstinate chastity, and Tarquin took his pleasure with her. Joyous and triumphant now that he had won the lady's beauty, he returned to the army.

How Lucretia killed herself and how her father, her husband, and her kin swore an oath on her blood (Ch. 48)

(par. 10) Lucretia was most sorrowful at the great wrong she had done,[17] and she soon sent a messenger to her father in Rome, and from there to Ardea and her husband, who was with the army; and she asked that each of them come to her quickly accompanied by a single, trusted companion, as there was great need and a dreadful thing had happened to her.[18] **(par. 11)** Her father, whose name was Spurius Lucretius,[19] along with his friend, called P[ublius] Valer[ius],[20] and her husband Collatine, along with the aforementioned [Lucius] Junius Brutus,[21] both of whom Lucretia's messenger had found in Rome, where they had come by chance[22] – they came to Collatia and found Lucretia, who was sitting in the midst of her chamber in great affliction. **(par. 12)** She gushed out tears when she saw her friends. And when her husband asked her if all their affairs were safe and sound, she said, "Not in the slightest. What affairs remain for a woman," she said, "when she has lost her chastity? Ah, Collatine," she said, "in your bed are the traces of a man, an outsider. My body has been raped and dishonored.[23] My heart is innocent of it, as my death shall attest. But in God's name give me your right hands and pledge your faith to me that the adulterer will suffer his punishment." **(par. 13)** She said, "It is Sextus Tarquinius who came to me as an enemy rather than a guest. For last night," she said, "he came to me fully armed and seized from me all joy and solace[24] – and also from himself, if you are men." **(par. 14)** The friends pledged their faith to her each one in turn, and then they comforted her sorrowful heart. And they told her that she had not sinned in the slightest, as she had been forced to do it,[25] and that it is the will that commits the sin not the body, and that where there is no consent there can be no guilt. **(par. 15)** Then Lucretia said to them, "You will soon

au corps qui se³⁹ est fourfait, car pour voir se il est⁴⁰ quipte de pechié pour ce ne voil je paz que il soit quipte de tourment, ne ne serrai example que nule non chaste fame doive vivre emprés moi." **(par. 16)** Donques a Lucrece le coutel, lequel celeement elle tenoit soz sa robe, fiché dedens son cuer et est cheue morte par dessus sa plaie. Si s'escrierent li maris et li perez et dementres que il se desconfortoient, Brutus li a trait le coutel de la plaie hors, et le tenens⁴¹ en presence du sanc qui decouroit a fet un serement et dit en ceste guise: "Par cesti sanc," dist il, "qui estoit tres chaste avant l'injure royal, c'est avant l'injure faite par le fil du roy, jure ge et promet a vous les dieux et vous en appele en tesmoing que je, par quelque force je⁴² porrai, executerai et destruirai par feu et par fer Tarquin l'orguilleus avecquez sa feme pleine de tout fourfait et toute la lignie⁴³ de leur enfans, ne ne soufferrai que nus d'ieux ni autrez regnet des hore mais a Rome." **(par. 17)** Li dessus diz Brutus a baillié le coutel a Collatin, et puis a Lucrecien et a Valerin dessus diz, si que eulz, mervillans dont tel engin estoit nouvelement nez eu piz du dit Brutus, ont juré et promis celle mesme promesse si come le dit Brutus leur commanda. Et tous convertis en ire et en courrous suirent le dit Bru [f. 19vd] tus, eulz appelant a destruire et a confondre celi royaume.

Comment le roy Tarquin et sa femme et ses enfans furent baniz de Rome .xlix. [Ch. 49]

(par. 18) Lors ont porté eu marché le corps Lucrece et ont esmeu les gens, si comme acoustumee chose est, ou pour cause de la nouveauté ou de horribleté de la chose. Et retorquoit⁴⁴ chascuns la besoingne en soi meismes en se plegnant de la force et de la iniquité royal, et lez perez aussi mout tristez, et aussi Brutus, qui blasmoit et chastioit lez autrez dont il plouroient, et leur disoit car trop mieux appartendroit aus homes romainz prendre armes contre ceulz qui osoient faire chosez si cruelez que plourer a guise de femez. **(par. 19)** Chascuns fiers homs a pris ses armez, et l'autre multitude des juvenceauz vait aprés et lessie⁴⁵ suffisant garnison en la cité de Collace et establies et mises gardes suffissantes es portes de celle a fin que nus n'alast a l'ost denoncier ceste chose au roy ne auz royaulz. Tous les autrez, armez avec Brutuz leur

---

    ³⁹ se *om. O*; corr. *GJ*. The *O* scribe has inserted a caret at this spot and added "se" in the left margin.
    ⁴⁰ est *om. O*; corr. *GJ*
    ⁴¹ lui tenant le coutel toullie de sanc et *G*
    ⁴² que je *G*
    ⁴³ ligniee *G*; lignee *J*
    ⁴⁴ recordoit *G*
    ⁴⁵ laissiee *G*; lessee *J*

see what we owe to a body that has committed a crime; for even if in truth it is free of sin, I do not wish it to be free of torment for that reason,[26] and I will not be an example that would suggest that an unchaste woman ought to live in imitating me." **(par. 16)** Then Lucretia thrust the knife, which she secretly held beneath her dress, into her heart, and she fell dead upon her wound. Then the husband and the father cried out, and while they gave in to despair, Brutus drew the knife out of the wound and holding it up in the presence of the blood dripping from it, he swore an oath and spoke in this way: "By this blood," he said, "which was very chaste before the royal offence, that is before the offence committed by the king's son,[27] I swear and promise to you, the gods, and call upon you as witnesses that I, with whatever force I may conjure, will apply the death sentence to Tarquin the Proud along with his wife, filled with every sin, and the entire lineage of their children and will make them perish by fire and the blade;[28] nor will I allow any of them or any other to reign henceforth in Rome." **(par. 17)** The above-mentioned Brutus handed the knife to Collatine, and then to Lucretius and to the above-mentioned Valerius, in such a way that they, marveling that such intelligence had newly sprung from the breast of said Brutus, swore and promised this same promise just as said Brutus commanded them. And with all of them turned to anger and wrath, they followed said Brutus, who called upon them to destroy and lay waste to this kingship.

How King Tarquin and his wife and his children were banished from Rome (Ch. 49)

(par. 18) Then, they carried Lucretia's body to the forum and stirred up the people there, as was bound to happen, either because of the unexpectedness of the thing or its frightfulness. And each man took this affair upon himself, complaining of royal violence and iniquity, as did the much-aggrieved father, and also Brutus, who reproached and denounced those who wept and said to them that it would be far more suitable for Roman men to take up arms against those who dared to do such cruel things than to weep in the manner of women.[29] **(par. 19)** Every bold man took up his arms, and the other multitude of young men goes after them,[30] having left a sufficient garrison in the city of Collatia and having established and placed enough guards at the gates of this city so that no one might head to the army to proclaim this state of affairs to the king or to other royals. All the other men, armed along with Brutus their

conduiseur, s'en sont venus a Rome. **(par. 20)** La ou il vindrent a Rome, quelque part que aloit la multitude armee fit paour et temoute. Et toutefois pour ce que on vooit ilecquez lez principaus de la cité, on pensoit bien que li movement n'estoit pas sanz cause, dont avint que la chose qui tant estoit cruele ne fit paz mendre movement a Rome que elle avoit fait a Collace. **(par. 21)** De par tous les lieuz donquez de la cité de Rome s'en court l'en[46] ou marchié, eu quel lieu comme on fust venus la crie a appelé le peuple au tribuin dez crimez, en quel office estoit lors Brutus. Eu quel lieu li dis Brutus a fait son oroison et son parlement au peuple, lequel n'aparut pas venir de celi piz, cest a dire de celi entendement ou de celi engin quel le dit Brutus avoit faint soy avoir jusquez a celi jour. **(par. 22)** Si a parlé Brutus de la violence et de la luxure de Sexte Tarquin, de la oppression outrageuse de Lucrece et de sa miserable mort, de la veveté Tricipitin, c'est le pere Lucrece, au quel on avoit doné cause et occasion de mort plus miserable que n'estoit la mort de sa fille. Et aussi parla il de l'orgueil du roy, et du labour et de la misere du peuple, que li dis roys avoit plungé en fousses et en cloaques expuisier, si que lez homes romains, victeurs[47] des autres homes, il avoit fait peyrres[48] et machons en lieu de batilleurs. Et si n'oblia pas a parler de la indigne mort du roy Serve Tulle, et comme sa cruele fille avoit son char fet passer sur son corps, a la quele chose vengier il appela les dieux qui vengent les parens. **(par. 23)** Cestes choses tant grieves et crueles et pluseurs autres (les quelez, je croi, que la enormité de cesti fait ne lessa pas reciter aus scripteurs), dictez et recordeez, il esmeut la multitude du peuple ardant et enflammee a ce que il privassent leur roy de son empire et que il commandassent[49] le roy Luce Tarquin et sa feme et ses enfans exiler du pays. **(par. 24)** Lors Brutus, esleuz [f. 20ra] et[50] armés les juvenceaus, qui a ce se offroient volunteirement, s'en ala a Ardee a fin de esmouvoir l'ost encontre le roy. Et lessa la segnorie de la cité de Rome a Lucretien dessus dit, qui par avant avoit esté fait preteur par le roy. La quele chose[51] oïe, la royne Tullie s›en fui a son hostel, et si la maudisoient tous ceulz par lez queles elle passoit, homez et femes, et requeroient[52] et apeloient[53] encontre lé[54] les furies d'enfer vengeressez de la mort des parens. **(par. 25)** Cestes choses denunceez en l'ost, li roys, tous effrayés comme de chose si nouvele, s'en vint tantost

---

[46] l'en *om. O*; corr. *GJ*
[47] vuteins *O*; corr. *GJ*
[48] pierreus *G*
[49] commdassent *O*; corr. *GJ*
[50] en *O*; corr. *GJ*
[51] chose *om. OJ*; corr. *G*
[52] requeroit *O*; corr. *G*
[53] appeloit *O*; corr. *G*
[54] li *G*

leader, went off to Rome. **(par. 20)** When they arrived at Rome, wherever the armed crowd went they caused fear and tumult. And yet since people saw the leaders of the city there, they thought that the uprising was not without cause, and so it came about that so cruel a thing did not cause a smaller uprising in Rome than it had caused in Collatia. **(par. 21)** Then, people come running from all parts of the city of Rome to the forum, and in that place, when they had arrived there, the crier summoned the people before the Tribune of Crimes,[31] which office Brutus then occupied. In that place, said Brutus made his speech and discourse to the people, one that did not seem to come from that breast – that is, from that understanding or from that intellect that aforementioned Brutus had pretended to possess up until that day. **(par. 22)** And Brutus spoke of the violence and of the lust of Sextus Tarquin, of the outrageous assault on Lucretia and of her miserable death, of [Spurius Lucretius] Tricipitinus's (that is, Lucretia's father's) loss of his daughter, Tricipitinus to whom had been given a cause and a reason for a death even more miserable than his daughter's death.[32] And he [Brutus] spoke also of the king's arrogance, and of the toil and misery of the people, whom said king had plunged into ditches and sewers to empty them out, just as he made Roman men, who were the vanquishers of other men, into stone-cutters[33] and masons rather than warriors. And he [Brutus] did not forget to speak of the disgraceful death of King Servius Tullius,[34] and of how his cruel daughter had had her chariot run over his body; and he called upon the gods who avenge parents to avenge this deed. **(par. 23)** Once these most grievous and cruel events and several others (which, I believe, the outrageousness of this conduct did not allow the chroniclers to recount) were described and recalled, he [Brutus] moved the crowd of fervent and inflamed people to the point that they deprived their king of his rule and ordered that King Lucius Tarquin and his wife and their children be exiled from the land. **(par. 24)** Then Brutus, having recruited and armed the youth, who voluntarily offered themselves up for this task, went off to Ardea in order to stir up the army against the king. And he left the command of the city of Rome to the aforementioned Lucretius, who previously had been made governor by the king.[35] When this thing was made known,[36] Queen Tullia fled her residence; and then all those she passed, men and women, cursed her and entreated and invoked against her the furies of hell, avengers of the death of parents. **(par. 25)** When these things were reported among the army, the king, deeply troubled by so unusual an event, soon made his way toward

vers Rome por apaisier et comprimer les mouvemens du peuple.[55] Et Brutus
l'a senti, si est destornés de son chemin a fin qu'il ne l'encontrast, et si que
en un meisme temps par diverses voies Brutus ala a l'ost a Ardee, et Tarquins
vint a Rome. Mes pour voir au roy furent closez lez portes et lui et ses enfans
exillez et bannis. Et le delivreur[56] de la cité, c'est a dire Brutus, fu liement
es[57] tentes receus. Et les deus enfans du roy qui erent demourés en l'ost si ont
suy leur pere et s'en alerent avecques lui en exil, en la cité de Cere, en pays
d'Etrurie. Et Sextes Tarquins s'en fuit en Gabie aussi comme en son regne,
eu quel lieu il a esté occis par les vengeurs des ancienez hainez, les queles il
avoit ilecquez jadis encouru[58] par les rapines et par les occisions, lez quelez
il avoit ilecquez jadis faites. **(par. 26)** Luces Tarquins li orguilleux regna a
Rome par l'espace de vint et cinc[59] ans. Et fu tout le temps que on a regné a
Rome, des le commencement jusquez a la delivrance de celle et a la expulsion
des roys, l'espace de deus cens et quarante et quatre ans. **(par. 27)** Lors a on
créé et esleu deus consuls por gouvrener la cité. Et furent ordené les comices,
c'est le temps de[60] eslire, par Lucretien[61] le Prefect, c'est le provost de la cité,
et furent esleus par lez centuriez selonc la forme de[62] l'ordenance que fit jadis
li roys Servius[63] Tullius, lez quelez consuls furent les dessus dis Junius Brutus
et Tarquins Collatins.[64]

Ci fenist li premiers livres de la premiere decade de Titus Livius.

[55]   peule *O*; corr. *J*
[56]   delivrer *O*; corr. *J*
[57]   en *O*; corr. *G*
[58]   deservies *O*
[59]   sinc *O*; corr. *J*
[60]   de *om. O*; corr. *GJ*
[61]   Lucien *O*; corr. *G*
[62]   fourme et *J*
[63]   Servilius *G*
[64]   collatif *GJO*

Rome to appease and contain the uprisings of the people. And Brutus heard of this and so changed his direction in order to avoid meeting him, such that at the same time but by different paths Brutus went to the army in Ardea and Tarquin came to Rome. But in truth the gates were closed to the king, and he and his children were exiled and banished.[37] And the liberator of the city, that is Brutus, was joyously received at the encampment.[38] And the two children of the king who were stationed with the army then followed their father and went with him into exile, in the city of Caere, in the land of Etruria.[39] And Sextus Tarquin fled to Gabii as if it were under his rule, at which place he was killed by the avengers of ancient hatreds, which he had formerly incurred in that place through lootings and killings that he had previously committed there.[40] **(par. 26)** Lucius Tarquin the Proud ruled in Rome over a space of twenty-five years. And the entire time that there were rulers in Rome, from its beginning up until its liberation and the expulsion of the kings, was a space of 244 years. **(par. 27)** They [the Romans] then elected and chose two consuls to govern the city. And the comitia,[41] that is, the time for elections, were established by Lucretius the Prefect, who was the governor of the city; and these [the consular comitia] were chosen by the centuriates in keeping with the form of the procedure that King Servius Tullius formerly created; and those consuls were the aforementioned Junius Brutus and Tarquin Collatine.[42]

Here ends the first book of the first decade of Titus Livius.

NOTES TO THE TRANSLATION

1   In general, we have indicated differences between Livy's text and Bersuire's in the translation rather than the edition, where the notes are limited to the signaling of variants and occasions when the control manuscripts were preferred to the base manuscript. Unless otherwise indicated, we cite Livy in the Loeb edition and translation: *Livy in Fourteen Volumes*, trans. B. O. Foster, vol. 1 (Books 1 and 2) (1919; Cambridge, MA: Loeb Classical Library, Harvard University Press, 1967), pp. 197–209.

2   Located twenty-two miles south of Rome, Ardea was the capital of the Rutuli, who were prominent members of the Latin League. The league was organized for the purpose of mutual defense, initially against the Etruscans and later against the Aequi and the Volsci.

3   Lucius Tarquinius Superbus, or Tarquin the Proud, was the seventh and last king of Rome. His twenty-five-year reign (534–509 BCE) was said to be so repressive that it justified the fall of the monarchy. We have emended our translation to include full and accurate proper names, adopting the spelling used in the Loeb edition and placing missing elements or corrections in brackets. Bersuire sometimes gives the Latin "Tarquinius" but more often reduces it to "Tarquin." He invariably reduces "Collatinus" to "Collatin," which we have rendered (following Shakespeare) as Collatine.

4   R. M. Ogilvie suggests another reason for the war: "Reluctant to accept Tarquin's high-handed usurpation of the [Latin] league, [Ardea] stood out against him and had to be reduced by force." See *A Commentary on Livy: Books 1–5* (Oxford: Clarendon Press, 1965), p. 220.

5   Tarquin imposed especially great burdens on the plebeians, who were not only obliged to build temples but also to dig the subterranean tunnel called the Cloaca Maxima, Rome's first sewer. When Tarquin no longer needed their labor, he sent many of them to the frontiers to serve as colonists. See *History of Rome* 1.56.1–3.

6   Bersuire translates *milites* ("soldiers") as *chevaliers* ("knights"), presumably without knowing that in ancient Rome the *equites* ("knights") were members of the wealthiest classes. See note 7 in the Verginia episode.

7   Livy names Sextus Tarquinius as the youngest of Lucius Tarquinius's three sons. See *History of Rome* 1.53.5.

8   Lucius Tarquinius Collatinus was a member of the royal family. His father, Arruns Tarquinius (known as Egerius, "the needy one," as he was left penniless when his father and grandfather died without leaving him an inheritance), was Tarquin the Proud's cousin. When Tarquin's father, Tarquinius Priscus, subdued the Latin town of Collatia, he sent Arruns to command a garrison there. Arruns's family then took their cognomen from the town. See Livy, *History of Rome* 1.34, 38.

9   Livy indicates here: "Let every man regard as the surest test what meets his eyes when the woman's husband enters unexpected" (1.57.7).

10   Bersuire seems to have added this sentence, which does not appear in Livy's text.

11   Collatia is thirteen miles east of Rome, meaning the ride was roughly thirty-five miles in total.

12   As Ogilvie notes, the Romans associated "the ideal of the *maman au foyer*…with the ritual symbol of wool-making which had originally been an economic necessity for the household and so symbolized all that a good household stood for, even when the practice was obsolete. The symbolism took concrete shape in the spindle and wool carried by a Roman bride," which signaled a relationship between *pudicitia*, "chastity, modesty, virtue," and *lanificia*, "the working of wool" (p. 222).

13   The women are presumably working in the semipublic atrium of a traditional Roman house.

14   Bersuire offers a considerable expansion of Livy, whose text reads, "It was there that Sextus Tarquinius was seized with a wicked desire to debauch Lucretia by force" (1.57.10). Livy's Tarquin does not imagine possibilities other than the use of force here.

15   This clause is missing from Livy's text.

16   Livy: "Then Tarquin began to declare his love" (1.58.3).

17   Bersuire uses an active voice construction, while Livy is more ambiguous, stating that Lucretia is "maesta tanto malo" (1.58.5), with the subject of "malo" not given. The Loeb translator sees the subject as Lucretia and gives us "grieving at her great disaster," though the clause could also be translated as "sorrowful at such an evil."

18   Livy does not specify the object of the terrible action but merely indicates that "a frightful thing had happened" (1.58.6).

19   Little is known of Spurius Lucretius beyond his role here and in a couple brief episodes from the early history of the Republic. Ogilvie suggests his character is likely "fictitious" (p. 229).

20   Publius Valerius came from a wealthy Sabine family that had settled in Rome soon after its founding. After the overthrow of the monarchy, he was elected consul and helped foil a plot by the exiled Tarquins to assassinate Collatine and Lucius Junius Brutus. Valerius was informed of the plot by a

slave named either Vindex or Vindicius. Livy claims that Vindex was rewarded with manumission and was the first slave to be freed through the touch of the *vindicta*. See Livy 2.5 and note 13 in the Verginia episode.

21 This is the first mention of Lucius Junius Brutus in this episode, though we find an extended portrait of him in the preceding episode. Brutus was the son of King Tarquin's sister and was horrified by his uncle's tyranny. Though shrewd and prudent, he pretended to be stupid ("brutus") while awaiting the chance to fight for freedom: "He carefully kept up the appearance and conduct of an idiot, leaving the king to do what he liked with his person and property, and did not even protest against his nickname of 'Brutus'; for under the protection of that nickname the soul which was one day to liberate Rome was awaiting its destined hour" (1.56.8).

22 Bersuire changes the emphasis in Livy's text, which reads, "Collatinus brought Lucius Junius Brutus, with whom he chanced to be returning to Rome when he was met by the messenger from his wife" (1.58.6).

23 Bersuire leaves out Livy's "only" here: "Yet my body only has been violated" (1.58.7).

24 In the Latin text (1.58.8), the joy (a fatal one: "pestiferum…gaudium") is Tarquin's alone, not Lucretia's, and there is no mention of solace.

25 Livy is more concise: the men "[divert] the blame from her who was forced to the doer of the wrong" (1.58.9).

26 Bersuire misreads Livy here and gives a harsher account of Lucretia than Livy does. In Livy, Lucretia declares, "It is for you to determine…what is due to him [quid illi debeatur]; for my own part, though I acquit myself of the sin, I do not absolve myself from punishment [supplicio]" (1.58.10). Bersuire wrongly takes the referent for "illi" as Lucretia's body rather than Tarquin. Then, he renders "supplicio" as "tourment," such that Lucretia calls for her body to receive not punishment but suffering.

27 Bersuire has added this clause as a gloss to Livy's "regiam iniuriam" (1.59.1).

28 Bersuire makes the threat more menacing. Livy's Brutus declares, "I will pursue Lucius Tarquinius Superbus and his wicked wife and all his children, with sword, with fire, aye with whatsoever violence I may" (1.59.1).

29 There is no explicit mention of women in Livy, only an indication that Brutus reproached the crowd for "their tears and idle lamentations and urged them to take up the sword, as befitted men and Romans" (1.58.4).

30 In Livy, these are all youths: "the boldest of the young men" go first, then "the others followed their example" (1.58.5).

31 Livy refers here to the *tribunus celerum*, or Tribune of the Celeres. The Celeres were the royal bodyguard, and their tribune commander was held to be second in authority only to the king. The role presumably fell to Brutus, as he was Lucius Tarquinius's nephew and the most senior member of the

royal household after the king and his sons, though Ogilvie casts doubt on the accuracy of this claim: "a man who had been regarded as half-witted would not have been entrusted with any responsible command" (p. 228). Bersuire seems to have misread *celerum* as *scelerum* and therefore translates *tribunus celerum* as "Tribune of Crimes."

32   Livy indicates that "in [Tricipitinus's] eyes the death of his daughter was not so outrageous and deplorable as was the cause of her death" (1.59.9).

33   We are aware of no other instance in Old or Middle French of the word *peyrre*, which is found in both mss. *O* and *J* and which Bersuire may have coined as a translation for Livy's *lapicida*, "stonecutter." The *G* manuscript proposes "pierreus," which is also unknown to us, though it is fairly close to perrier, "quarryman."

34   Bersuire's translation is a bit loose here. In the Latin text, this event was recalled ("memorata") by Brutus (1.59.10). Livy's account of the life and death of Servius Tullius, the semilegendary sixth king of Rome, is found in *History of Rome* 1.39–48. Born to a Latin noblewoman who had been seized and enslaved by the Romans, Servius grew up in the royal household where he was recognized as a future leader by the miraculous appearance of a ring of fire over his head as he slept. He eventually married into the royal family and acceded to the throne when his father-in-law, Lucius Tarquinius Priscus, was assassinated in an attempted coup. Servius had a long reign and was celebrated for legal, political, and economic reforms that would later be seen as anticipating republican values. He was himself assassinated. His son-in-law, the future Tarquin the Proud, goaded on by his wife, Servius's daughter and the future Queen Tullia, denounced Servius to the Senate as a slave who favored the poor over the wealthy. When Servius appeared to defend himself, Tarquin had him murdered and left the corpse to rot in the streets. Tullia later drove her chariot over her father's body.

35   Livy names Lucretius *praefectus urbis*, as does Tacitus in the *Annals* 6.11. However, Ogilvie doubts the office existed in the regal period: "The title implies a distinction between *urbs* and *ager Romanus* which is unrealistic at this date. Besides, Sp. Lucretius himself is of dubious historicity" (p. 229).

36   Livy has instead, "During this confusion" (1.59.13).

37   Livy makes no mention of the children. Tarquin alone is exiled from Rome, though his children are driven out of the encampment.

38   Bersuire uses *tentes* as a synecdoche for a military encampment and as a translation for *castra* or "camp."

39   Caere is the Latin name for Caisra, an Etruscan town located approximately thirty-five miles northwest of Rome, in southern Etruria.

40   We learn the reason for the Gabians' hatred in *History of Rome* 1.53–54. Sextus Tarquinius helps obtain a victory for Rome by pretending to defect from the army in disgust at his father's arrogance and cruelty. He takes refuge

in Gabii, earns the Gabians' trust, and then arranges for the execution of their most eminent citizens.

[41]   Bersuire defines *comice* in his glossary; see note 54 in the Verginia episode. He uses the word in two distinct ways in this sentence, referring, first, to the time of year when Romans elected magistrates and public officers and, second, to the results of those elections, here, the appointment of consuls.

[42]   Bersuire adds explanatory material to this final paragraph, some of it inaccurate. Livy: "Two consuls were then chosen in the centuriated comitia [comitiis centuriatis], under the presidency of the Prefect of the City, in accordance with the commentaries of Servius Tullius. These were Lucius Junius Brutus and Lucius Tarquinius Collatinus" (1.60.3–4). The *comitia centuriata* was the electoral assembly, not, as Bersuire supposes, the time for elections. See note 81 in the Verginia episode.

Figure 11   Lucretia is accosted in her bed by Tarquin the Proud, *Tite-Live*.
A privately held Lillois manuscript, ca. 1470, f. 40v.
Courtesy Dr. Jörn Günther Rare Books, Basel (Switzerland).

ore fu luctesse monlt tviftett
f dolante de grant mal toe
ell auont fait Et emoia ta
toft bon message a comme a son pve
et Oileagnes a gaudte a son marv

Figure 12   Lucretia prepares to commit suicide with a dagger, *Tite-Live*.
A privately held Lillois manuscript, ca. 1470, f. 41v.
Courtesy Dr. Jörn Günther Rare Books, Basel (Switzerland).

3

The Tale of Verginia from Jean de Meun's
Roman de la rose

We have chosen as the base manuscript for our edition of this short text a late thirteenth-century manuscript that has not been previously edited, Dijon ms. 526 (Ernest Langlois's ms. *Ca*). This manuscript is known for collecting works by Richard de Fournival along with the *Rose*. It was produced by a Picard scribe and features numerous spellings from his dialect. We have used ms. BnF fr. 1573 (Langlois's ms. *Ab*) as a control manuscript.

Lady Reason, during her discussion with the Lover in the opening scene of Jean de Meun's continuation of Guillaume de Lorris's open-ended *Rose*, attempts to convert him to a generalized notion of love as a kind of Christian charity, as opposed to his erotic attraction to the rose – in other words, a love toward everyone as opposed to the passionate love of one person. After telling the tale of the castration of Saturn by Jupiter, the birth of Venus, and the subsequent departure of Justice from the earth, Reason argues that if Love were universally present, there would be no need for Justice, since there would be no crimes. However, Justice alone would destroy the world if charitable love were to disappear.

[f. 68v]

[If charitable love were shared by all] paisivle[1] et koi
trestuit chil[2] del monde vivroient;
jamais roi ne prince n'aroient,
sergans, ne baillius,[3] ne prevos;
dont vivroit li pueples devos.
Jamais juges n'orroit[4] clamours,
dont di je ke mius vaut amours
simplement ke ne fait justice,
tout[5] voist[6] ele encontre malice,
ki fu mere des signouries,
dont les francises sont peries.
Car, se ne fust mals et pechiés,
dont li mondes est entechiés,
on n'euïst onques rois eüs
n'en terre juges cogneüs,
si se pruevent il malement.
Il deuïssent premierement
Els meïsmes justefiier,
puis k'on se velt en els fiier,
et loiaus estre et diligent,
ne mie laske et negligent,
ne couvoiteus, faus, et faintis,
pour faire droiture as plaintis.
Mais or vendent les jugemens
et bestournent les erremens,
et taillent et comptent et raient,[7]
et les boines gens trestout paient.
Tuit s'efforcent de l'autrui prendre.
Tels juges fait les larçons pendre
qui mius devroit estre pendus,
se jugemens en fust rendus
des rapines et des torffais
k'il a par son pooir fourfais.

[If charitable love were shared by all,] everyone in the world would live in peace and tranquility; they would never have a king or a prince, nor men-at-arms, nor bailiffs, nor provosts; and for that reason, people would live respectfully. A judge would never hear complaints, which is why I say that Love is simply worth more than Justice, however much she [Justice] fights against Evil, who was the mother of lordships, on account of which freedoms have been destroyed. Indeed, if it were not for evil and sin, with which the world is stained, we would never have had a king nor known a judge on earth, and yet they prove themselves poorly in this endeavor. Before anything else they ought to display their own righteousness, since people want to have trust in them, and they ought to be trustworthy and diligent, not cowardly and negligent, nor covetous, false, and deceitful, in order to render justice to plaintiffs. Yet now they sell their judgments, and turn their procedures upside down, and gather their fees, pad their accounts, and make erasures, and good people pay for every bit of it. They all make an effort to steal others' goods. Such a judge has thieves hanged when he would have better deserved to be hanged, if a judgment had been rendered against him for the rapines and torts he used his power to commit.

En ne fist bien Appius a pendre,
qui fist a son sergant emprendre
par faus tesmoing fausse querele
contre Virgine la pucele,
qui fu fille Virginius,
si com dist Titus Livius,
qui bien seit le cas raconter
pour chou k'il ne pooit donter
le pucele qui n'avoit cure
ne de lui ne de sa luxure?
Li ribaus dist en audience,
"Sires juges, donnés sentence
pour moi, car li pucele est moie.
Pour me serve le prouveroie
contre tous chiaus qui sont en vie,
car, ou k'ele ait esté nourrie,
en mon hosteil me fu emblee
des lors, par Diu,[8] k'ele fu nee
et baillie a Virginium.
Si vous requier, sire Appium,
ke vous me delivrés me serve,
car bien est drois k'ele me serve,
nompas celui que l'a nourrie.
Et se Virginius le nie,
tout che sui je pres de prouver,
car boins tesmoins en puis trouver."
Ensi parloit li mals trahistres,
qui del faus juge estoit menistres,
et com li plais ensi alast,
ains ke Virginius parlast,
qui tous pres estoit de respondre
pour ses adversaires confondre,
juga par hastive sentence
Appius ke sans attendance
Fust li pucele au serf rendue.
Et quant le cose a entendue,
li beau[9] preudom devant nommés,
boins chevaliers bien renommés,
c'est a savoir Virginius,
ke bien voit ke vers Appius
ne puet pas sa fille deffendre,
ains li couvient par force rendre,

8   foi *Ab*
9   boins *Ca*; corr. *Ab*

Did Appius not deserve to hang? According to Livy, who knows well how to recount these events, Appius had his servant submit a false complaint based on false testimony against the maiden Verginia, who was the daughter of Verginius, because Appius was unable to subdue the maiden, who had no interest in him or his lechery. The scoundrel said before the court: "Lord judge, render judgment in my favor, for the maiden is mine. I would prove her to be my slave against any man alive; for regardless of where she was raised, I swear to God she was stolen from me out of my house just after she was born and was given to Verginius. So I entreat you, lord Appius, to hand my slave over to me, for it is only right that she serve me, not he who raised her. And if Verginius denies it, I am prepared to prove all of this, for I am able to find good witnesses in the matter."

Thus spoke the wicked traitor, who was a servant to the treacherous judge; and as the case proceeded in this way, before Verginius could speak (he was well prepared to respond and confound his adversaries), Appius made a hasty ruling whereby the maiden was to be given to the servant without delay. And when the fine and worthy man I just mentioned, Verginius, a good knight with a fine reputation, heard what had happened, and when he saw clearly that he had no way to defend his daughter against Appius but had to surrender her by force and

et son cors livrer a hontage,
si change[10] honte pour carnage
par mervilleus appensement,
se Titus Livius ne ment,
car il par amour sans haïnne
a sa bele fille Virgine
tantost a le teste coupee
et puis au juge presentee
devant tous en plain concitoire.
Et li juges, selonc l'ystoire,
le commanda tantost a prendre
pour lui mener occirre ou pendre,
mais nel occist ne ne pendi,
car li pueples le deffendi,
[f. 69r]
Qui tous fu de pitié meüs
si tost com li fais fu seüs.
Puis fu pour ceste mesprison
Appius mis en fort prison
et s'occist la hastivement,
ains le jour de son jugement.
Et Claudius, li calengieres,
fu jugiés a mort comme leres
se ne l'en[11] eüist respitié
Virginius, par sa pitié,
qui tant vaut le pueple proier
k'en essil[12] le fist[13] envoier.
Et trestout chil[14] dampné morurent
qui de se cause tesmoing furent.

[10]   canga *Ca*; corr. *Ab*
[11]   son nel *Ca*; corr. *Ab*
[12]   escilg *Ca*; corr. *Ab*
[13]   vaut *Ca*; corr. *Ab*
[14]   chilg *Ca*; cil *Ab*

deliver her body to disgrace, he had an inspired thought for how to exchange shame for butchery, if Livy does not lie. For Verginius swiftly cut off the head of his beautiful daughter Verginia, not out of hatred but out of love, and then presented it to the judge before everyone in open court.

And as the story goes, the judge immediately ordered that he be seized and taken off to be killed or hanged. Yet Appius neither killed nor hanged him, for the people, who were moved to great pity as soon as the deed was made known, defended him. Appius was then thrown in a fortified prison for this miscarriage of justice, and he promptly killed himself there before the day of his trial. And Claudius, the false accuser, was sentenced to death as a thief and would thus have died if Verginius had not spared him out of pity: he was so intent on imploring the people that he had him sent into exile. And all those who were witnesses on his behalf, having been condemned, were put to death.

Q uc bien fait le faut raconptcr:
D our ce âl ne muoit fommtcr·

Figure 13 Verginia's trial and death, *Roman de la rose*. The Bodleian
Libraries, University of Oxford, Douce 195, f. 41r.

Figure 14 Verginius beheads Verginia, *Roman de la rose*. Bibliothèque
nationale de France, Département des Manuscrits, Français 380, f. 38v.

4

The Tale of Lucretia from Jean de Meun's
Roman de la rose

We have chosen as the base manuscript for our edition of this short text a late thirteenth-century manuscript that has not been previously edited, Dijon ms. 526 (Ernest Langlois's ms. *Ca*). This manuscript is known for collecting works by Richard de Fournival along with the *Rose*. It was produced by a Picard scribe and features numerous spellings from his dialect. We have used ms. BnF fr. 1573 (Langlois's ms. *Ab*) as a control manuscript.

Jean de Meun assigns the story of Lucretia to the Jealous Husband, who inserts it into a misogynous attack on unfaithful wives: if a married woman is rich or beautiful, all men go after her; and if she is ugly, she tries to please everyone, so it is difficult for a husband to fight against all her suitors. The Jealous Husband treats Lucretia, along with Penelope, as an exception who proves the rule that all women yield willingly to seduction.

[f. 85r]

Et comment porroit nuls che faire
K'il gart cose ke tuit guerroient
Ou qui velt tous chiaus qui le voient?
S'il prent a tout le monde guerre,
Il n'a pooir de vivre en terre.
Dehors istront pour estre[1] prises,
Pour tant ke soient bien requises.
Penelope neïs prendroit
Qui bien a li prendre entendroit,
Si n'eut il milleur dame en Grece.
Si feroit il, par Diu!, Lucrece[2],
Ja soit chou k'el se soit[3] ochise,
Pour chou k'a force l'avoit prise
Li fils au roi Tarquinius.[4]
Pour chou, dist Tytus Livius,[5]
Maris ne peres ne parens
Ne li porent estre garans,
Pour paine ke nuls i mesist,
Ke devant ials ne s'ochesist.
Dou duel laissier molt li requisent:
Molt de beles raisons li disent,
Et ses maris meïsmement
Le confortoit piteusement
Et de boin cuer li pardonnoit
Tout le fait et li sermonnoit
Et s'estudioit a trouver
Vives raisons pour li prouver
Ke ses cors n'avoit pas pechié
Quant ses cuers ne vaut le pechié,
Car cors ne puet estre pechieres
Se li cuers n'en est consentieres.
Mais ele, qui son duel menoit,
Un coutel en sa main[6] tenoit,
Repuns, ke nuls ne le veïst

[1] D. ...estre] Nus nes garderoit d'estre p.] *Ab*
[2] Lutrece *Ca*; corr. *Ab*
[3] kele soit *Ca*; corr. *Ab*
[4] Tarquinus *Ca*; corr. *Ab*
[5] chivilivius *Ca*; corr. *Ab*
[6] sain *Ab*

And how could anyone manage to keep an individual whom all men are fighting to conquer or who wants all those who see her? If he wages war against the entire world, he does not have the power to survive on earth. They will go outside in order to be taken, provided that they are well wooed. A man who was intent upon taking possession of her could even capture Penelope, although there was no better lady in Greece. By God, he could even do so with Lucretia, even though she killed herself because the son of King Tarquin took her by force. For as Livy recounted, neither husband nor father nor kinsman could prevent her from killing herself in front of them, no matter how much effort any of them put into it. They implored her greatly to abandon her grief and offered her many good reasons. Even her husband comforted her compassionately. With all his heart he forgave her the entire matter and exhorted her, devoting himself to find keen arguments to prove to her that her body had not sinned when her heart did not desire the sin. For a body cannot be a sinner if the heart does not consent to it. Yet she, whose grief ruled her, was holding a knife in her hand, hidden from view so that none could see it

Quant pour soi ferir le preïst,
Si leur respondi sans vergoigne:
"Biau signeur, qui ke me pardoigne
L'ort pechié dont si fort me poise,
Ne comment ke du pardon voise,
Je ne pardonne pas le painne."
Lors fiert de grant angoisse plaine
Son cuer, si le fent, si se porte
Devant els a le terre morte.
Mais ains pria qu'il travillaissent
Tant por li ke se mort vengaissent.
Chest exemple vauch procurer
Pour les femes asseürer
Ke nuls a forche nes eüst
Qui de mort morir ne deüst,
Dont li rois et ses fils en furent
Mis en escil[7] et i morurent.
N'onc[8] puis roumain par cel desroi
Ne vaurrent faire a Romme roi.
S'en est il pau tels com[9] Lucrece[10]
Ne com Penelope de Grece[11].

  [7]   escilg *Ca*; corr. *Ab* (essil)
  [8]   Non *Ca*; corr. *Ab*
  [9]   Si nest il mes nule *Ab*
  [10] Lutrece *Ca*; corr. *Ab*
  [11] Ne P. nule en G. *Ab*

when she took it to stab herself. She responded thus to them without shame: "Fair lords, whoever should forgive me the vile sin that weighs on me so heavily, and no matter what pardon might be granted, I do not forego the punishment." Then, filled with great agony, she struck herself in the heart and split it, bringing herself to the ground before them, dead. Before that, she implored that they work so hard for her cause that they avenge her death. She wished to establish this exemplary tale to reassure women that no man would have them by force who was not obliged to die a certain death. As a result, the king and his son were sent into exile and died there. Never since, as a result of this arrogance, have the Romans wished to give Rome a king. Nonetheless, there are few women like Lucretia, and few like Penelope in Greece.

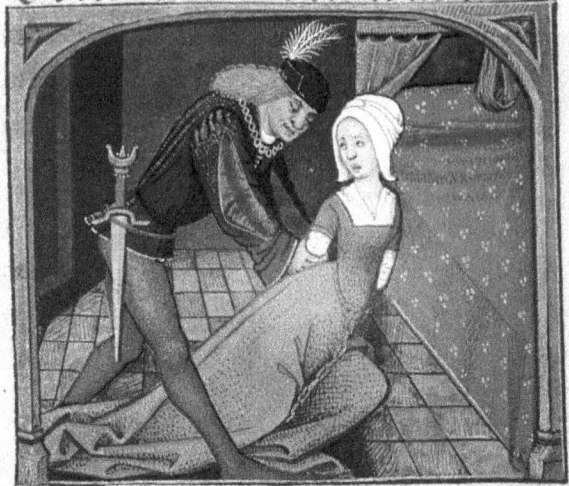

Figure 15 Lucretia's rape, *Roman de la rose*. The Bodleian Libraries, University of Oxford, Douce 195, f. 61v.

Figure 16 Lucretia's suicide, *Roman de la rose*, Bibliothèque nationale de France, Département des Manuscrits, Français 12595, f. 64v.

BIBLIOGRAPHY

Editions, Translations, and Images

Brucker, Charles. *Anthologie commentée des traductions françaises du XIVe siècle: Autour de Charles V (culture, pouvoir et spiritualité)*, vol. 1, 334–42. Paris: Champion, 2020. Edition of brief excerpts from the *Tite-Live*, including the authorial prologue, which precedes the translation of the first decade, and a passage on the origins of the Second Punic War, which is the beginning of the first book of the second decade. Bersuire's second decade corresponds to Livy's third, as the latter's second decade was unknown in the Middle Ages and thus not included in Bersuire's translation.

Histoire romaine de Tite-Live: Traduction française de Pierre Bersuire: Reproduction des 63 miniatures des manuscrits français 273 et 274 de la Bibliothèque nationale. Paris: Berthaud Frères and Catala Frères, 1907.

Meyer, Paul, editor. *Documents manuscrits de l'ancienne littérature de la France conservés dans les bibliothèques de la Grande-Bretagne*, 81–82. Paris: Imprimerie nationale, 1871. Edition of the opening of the authorial prologue to the *Tite-Live* in both French and Catalan.

Tesnière, Marie-Hélène. *Le livre IX des "Décades" de Tite-Live traduites par Pierre Bersuire, suivi du commentaire de Nicolas Trivet*. Diplôme d'archiviste paléographe, École nationale des chartes, 1977.

———. "À propos de la traduction de Tite-Live par Pierre Bersuire: Le manuscrit Oxford, Bibliothèque Bodléienne, Rawlinson C447." *Romania* 118 (2000): 449–98. Edition of Bersuire's glossary to the *Tite-Live* (485–98).

Wittlin, Curt J., editor. *Titus Livius: Ab urbe condita I.1–9: Ein mittellateinischer Kommentar und sechs romanische Übersetzungen und Kürzungen aus dem Mittelalter aus den Handschriften*. Romanische Paralleltexte 2. Tübingen: Max Niemeyer, 1970. Edition of Livy 1.1–9 along with Trevet's Latin adaptation and four vernacular translations: Bersuire's French translation, an anonymous Catalan translation, Pero López de Ayala's Spanish translation, and an anonymous Italian translation.

Further Reading

Duval, Frédéric. "*Ab urbe condita libri CXLII*, T. Livius: Traduction de Pierre Bersuire (achevée en septembre 1358." *Miroir des Classiques*. Élec (Éditions en ligne de l'École des chartes). http://elec.enc.sorbonne.fr/miroir_ des_classiques/xml/classiques_latins/ab_urbe_condita_cxlii_titus-livius. xml#bersuire.

———. "Le glossaire de traduction, instrument privilégié de la transmission du savoir: Les *Decades* de Tite-Live par Pierre Bersuire." In *La transmission des savoirs au Moyen Âge et à la Renaissance, Vol. 1: Du XIIe au XVe siècle*, edited by Pierre Nobel, 43–64. Besançon: Presses universitaires de Franche-Comté, 2005.

Krynen, Jacques. "Entre la réforme et la révolution: Paris, 1356–1358." In *Les révolutions françaises: Les phénomènes révolutionnaires en France*, edited by Frédéric Bluche, 87–112. Paris: Fayard, 1989.

Monfrin, Jacques. *Études de philologie romane*. Publications romanes et françaises 230. Geneva: Droz, 2001. Reprints "Humanisme et traductions au Moyen Âge" (757–85) and "Les traducteurs et leur public en France au Moyen Âge" (787–801), cited below.

———. "Humanisme et traductions au Moyen Âge," *Journal des Savants* no. 3 (July–September 1963): 161–90.

———. "La première traduction française de Tite-Live." In *Bulletin de la Société Nationale des Antiquaires de France, 1958*, 82–85. Paris: Klincksieck, 1959.

———. "Les traducteurs et leur public au Moyen Âge." *Journal des savants* no. 1 (January–March 1964): 5–20.

Pannier, Léopold. "Notice biographique sur le bénédictin Pierre Bersuire, premier traducteur de Tite-Live." *Bibliothèque de l'École des Chartes* 33 (1872): 325–64.

Rychner, Jean. "Observations sur la traduction de Tite-Live par Pierre Bersuire (1354–1356)." *Journal des savants* 4 (1963): 242–67.

Samaran, Charles. "Pierre Bersuire, prieur de Saint-Éloi de Paris." *Histoire littéraire de la France* 39 (1962): 259–450. The section on "La traduction française de Tite-Live" (358–414) is by Jacques Monfrin, who also contributed to the appendix (434–50, a bibliography of manuscripts and editions).

Scala, Elizabeth. "Did Chaucer Know Livy?" *Notes and Queries* 68 (2021): 255–58.

Sinclair, K. V. *The Melbourne Livy. A Study of Bersuire's Translation Based on the Manuscript in the Collection of the National Gallery of Victoria*. Australian Humanities Research Council 7. Melbourne University Press, 1961.

Tesnière, Marie-Hélène. "Les *Décades* de Tite-Live traduites par Pierre Bersuire et la politique éditoriale de Charles V." In *Quand la peinture était dans les livres: Mélanges en l'honneur de François Avril à l'occasion de la remise du titre de docteur honoris causa de la Freie Universität Berlin*, edited by Mara Hofmann and Caroline Zöhl, 345–52. Ars Nova 15. Turnhout and Paris: Brepols and Bibliothèque nationale de France, 2007.

———. "Un manuscrit exceptionnel des *Décades* de Tite-Live traduites par Pierre Bersuire." In *La traduction vers le moyen français: Actes du IIe colloque de l'AIEMF, Poitiers, 27–29 avril 2006*, edited by Claudio Galderisi and Cinzia Pignatelli, 125–47. Medieval Translator 11. Turnhout: Brepols, 2007.

———. "Pierre Bersuire, traducteur des *Décades* de Tite-Live: Nouvelles perspectives." In *Quand les auteurs étaient des nains: Stratégies auctoriales des traducteurs français de la fin du Moyen Âge*, edited by Olivier Delsaux and Tania Van Hemelryck, 113–58. Turnhout: Brepols, 2019.

———. "À propos de la traduction de Tite-Live par Pierre Bersuire: Le manuscrit Oxford, Bibliothèque Bodléienne, Rawlinson C447." *Romania* 118 (2000): 449–98.

———."Un remaniement du *Tite-Live* de Pierre Bersuire par Laurent de Premierfait (manuscrit Paris, B.N., fr. 264–265–266)." *Romania* 107 (1986): 231–81.

———. "Une traduction des *Décades* de Tite-Live pour Jean le Bon," *Revue de la Bibliothèque nationale de France* 23 (2006): 81–85.

Veysseyre, Géraldine. "La *Fleur des histoires* de Jean Mansel: Une réception de Tite-Live à travers la traduction de Pierre Bersuire." In *Textes et cultures: Réception, modèles, interférences: Volume 1: Réception de l'antiquité*, edited by Pierre Nobel, 119–43. Besançon: Presses universitaires de Franche-Comté, 2004.

Wittlin, Curt J. "Tite-Live, Trevet, Bersuire: Un exemple de l'importance des commentaires médiévaux pour les premiers traducteurs." *The Humanities Association Review* 28, no. 3 (Summer 1977): 217–31.

INDEX

Gallica
Already Published

www.ingramcontent.com/pod-product-compliance
Ingram Content Group UK Ltd.
Pitfield, Milton Keynes, MK11 3LW, UK
UKHW031539100125
453394UK00008B/134

9 781843 847359